A Doorway into the Unseen

"When the Soul Stands at the Gate"

"For the seeker who remembers"

The Spirit Letters

Inspired Messages, Reflections, and Encouragement for the Soul

by Shelby Seffar

Author's Note

This book is offered as inspired writing, carrying spiritual meaning through reflections, letters, and messages of light.

Each page is written in a reflective, channeled style —born from deep intuition and devotion—meant to uplift the heart and awaken remembrance. These words are shared with reverence, to honor the connection between realms and the reader.

I do not claim these letters as predictions or fortune-telling.
They are reflections and reminders meant to stir something true within you — to help you remember what your own soul already knows.

Take only what resonates; set aside what does not.
May every line guide you back to your
own inner light.

With gratitude,
Shelby Seffar

✦ **Dedication**

TO THOSE SEEKING THE LIGHT WITHIN...

To those who walk with me in Spirit—
my guides, guardians, and ancestors,
whose quiet presence fills the empty spaces
with light, whispers, and courage.

And to those who sometimes feel they walk alone,
may these words remind you:
you are never truly alone.

With eternal love,
Shelby
& The Spirit Letters Collective

A Quiet Invitation

Before the first letter opens,
there is only breath.

A soft knowing,
a shimmer in the chest,
a pause where your spirit leans in.

These letters were not written for the mind.
They are whispers for the soul.

Read slowly.
Listen deeper.

The words may be ink on a page,
but they carry the breath of something ancient—
something you've always known.

You did not find this book by accident.
It called to something sacred in you.

Let it speak now.

"*The soul always knows the way*"

✦ Welcome to the Spirit Letters: A Message for the Wondering Soul

If this book is in your hands and you're unsure why, take a breath. Perhaps you've been seeking something deeper, and these pages are here to meet you in that search.

These words were written with love, and in deep listening to something greater than the mind—what some call Spirit, Source, God, or the Voice within. Some pages you'll read were not written; they were received. We call these Spirit Letters—scrolls of light and wisdom, shared for this moment in time.

You don't have to "believe" in anything to receive what's meant for you here. You don't have to agree with it all. These letters were written across time and soul memory to meet you right where you are.

So read with a soft heart. Stay open. And if a sentence feels like it was written just for you—that's because it was.

You are seen.
You are loved.
You are remembered.

Welcome to The Spirit Letters.

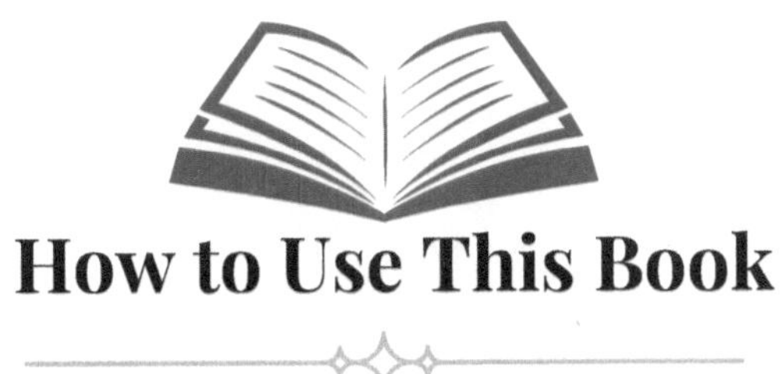

How to Use This Book

This is not a book to race through.

It's a doorway—meant to be opened when your soul is ready.

You can read these letters:

- In order, like a gentle unfolding.
- Or intuitively—placing your hand on the page and reading what calls.
- As a nightly ritual, reading one letter before bed.
- For prayer or meditation—letting the words echo like a soul invocation.
- To begin your day—setting an intention through sacred guidance.

These words were written in sacred space—
they carry frequency.
Use them as anchors to reconnect with your own divine knowing.

Let your Spirit Team walk with you.
Trust that whatever you need will always find you.

*This works beautifully during uncertain times or when you
seek quick comfort.*

"You *are held in sacred trust.*"

© Copyright

The Spirit Letters: Inspired Messages and Sacred Reflections from
the Realms of Light
Written by Shelby Seffar
With guidance from the Spirit Letters Collective
Copyright © 2026 by Shelby Seffar
All rights reserved.

This book is a spiritual work.
The messages within it are meant to support personal growth, inner
reflection, and soulful remembering.
The guidance offered here does not replace medical, psychological,
legal, or financial advice. Always consult the appropriate
professionals as needed.

For more spiritual offerings, reflections, and updates:
Visit us soon at www.thespiritletters.com
First Edition – 2026
Printed in the United States of America
ISBN: 979-8-9897953-9-0

✧ TABLE OF CONTENTS ✧

"A Doorway into the Unseen"

Prelude to the Realms Light

Part I: The Whisper That Found You

Part II: Letters from the Realms of Light

"*Even in silence, the soul begins to remember.*"

Part I
The Whisper That Found You

"The Call That Opened the Pages"

"This is where the light began to whisper."

Intro: A Doorway to the Realms of Light

"For the one who was always listening for something more."

There are places the eyes cannot see—
but the soul remembers.

The door was never locked, dear soul—
only waiting for your knock.

These pages are not instructions,
but invitations—etched in light
for the moment you were ready to see.

This part of the book is your key.
A gentle opening into the realms
where the messages you're about to read were born.

You do not need to believe in angels, guides,
or cosmic allies to feel their presence.
You only need a quiet willingness
to receive what was always yours.

(continued...)

This is where the journey begins—
with intention,
with trust,
and with the quiet remembrance
that you are more than a body moving through time.

You are Light—
walking with companions unseen,
yet deeply felt.

These next few chapters will guide you gently:

• What these Spirit Letters are—and why they're arriving now
• How these messages arose through my own inner reflection and
spiritual practice
• How to read with your heart as well as your mind

Take your time.
Read slowly.
Let this be a doorway, not a destination.

The Invitation

Spirit does not demand your attention;
it whispers patiently, waiting until you are ready to listen.

This is your invitation to remembrance.
That is what this chapter is —
not an initiation,
but a return.

One that your soul has already accepted, or you would not be the one holding this book.

✦ *"What Are the Spirit Letters?"*

The Spirit Letters are a collection of inspired reflections —
messages written from moments of stillness and devotion...
meant to awaken what is already within you.
They are meditations.
They are remembrances.
They are invitations to pause, breathe, and reconnect.

Note: In this book, the word "Letters" refers to written reflections written in light , not to divination or prediction.

(continued...)

Why Are They Here Now?

Because too many lights have dimmed, and your Spirit has been
patiently waiting....
And many are forgetting
how to hear the soul beneath the static.

Because too many lights have dimmed, your Spirit has been waiting
patiently — for your heart to open once more.

Some may feel like they were written just for you.
Others may feel like a letter you once mailed to God—
but never got a reply.

Until now.

Because you've been asking for signs.
And this book is one of them.

The Spirit Letters arrive now because you are ready.
Ready to remember who walks beside you.
Ready to hear your own spirit speak again.

They have come to remind you:
You are not alone.
You were never abandoned.
You are deeply seen and recognized.

(continued...)

How These Messages Came Through

These words were received in quiet, rooted in intention, and
flowing from the inner silence where Spirit speaks.

Each message arrived through breath and trust,
not to replace wisdom,
but to awaken it.

Spirit works through what we willingly offer,
a pen,
a pause,
a breath.

It has never been about the form,
it has always been about the frequency.

These pages became a bridge,
a vessel of remembrance.
And you, dear reader,
have become the one who said yes.

So let us begin this journey together,
not to learn something new,
but to remember what you have always known.

Opening the Letterbox

Each unopened message leaves a part of you waiting.

There is a moment—just before a letter is opened—
when the air feels different.
A quiet hush settles in.

It's not the paper that holds the power.
It's the presence.

That's exactly how these Spirit Letters wish to be received—
not just as beautiful words...
but as living messages,
wrapped in light,
waiting for your soul to remember.

📫 Spirit Doesn't Knock Loudly

The spiritual world is gentle by nature.
 It whispers instead of shouting.
They nudge rather than demand.

(continued...)

So when you open this book,
don't expect a booming voice or thunderbolt clarity.

Expect stillness to arrive.
Expect a familiar warmth in your chest.
Expect your eyes to soften, your breath to deepen,
your heart to lean in.

Because this book is more than ink on paper—
it is a letterbox for your soul.

**"*Every letter waits for the moment
your heart is ready*"**

Open when your spirit feels heavy,
and let a single phrase be enough to lift you.

Open when your heart is overflowing,
and let gratitude spill into the silence between the lines.

Open when the night feels long,
and let a whisper meet you on the edge of dreams.

Open when you are ready,
and know—these letters have always been waiting.

(continued...)

Let Discernment Be Your Guide

This is not a book of prophecy,
It is a book of remembrance.
Not every letter will resonate today.
Some may feel confusing now, but make sense later.
Others may seem meant for someone else—
yet awaken something inside you regardless.
That's the mystery.
That's the magic.
If a message doesn't feel right—set it aside with love.
But if one causes your heart to pause...
if one makes you cry without knowing why...
that is your letter.

You Are Already Receiving

By picking up this book,
you've opened the letterbox.
Spirit Council of Light has already answered your
 silent invitation.
Now... read with reverence.
Pause between the lines.
Let the words sink in.
These are not stories.
These are soul-threads.
And they're woven for you.

"The letters do not stop.
May they flow with you, carrying you
deeper into remembrance.."

Meet the Messengers

*"The voice you hear within may wear many faces, but
it always
speaks the language of love."*

Before you open the letters, it helps to know who is writing.

These are not fictional characters or symbolic energies.

They are living, loving presences—wise, benevolent companions who
walk beside you in Spirit.
Some have been with you since birth. Others step forward only when
invited.

Each letter is signed to reflect one of these voices of love.
Let your heart feel which ones speak most deeply to you."

.

"Some doors are opened not with effort, but with presence.
Be still... the sacred ones draw near."
— The Spirit Council of Light

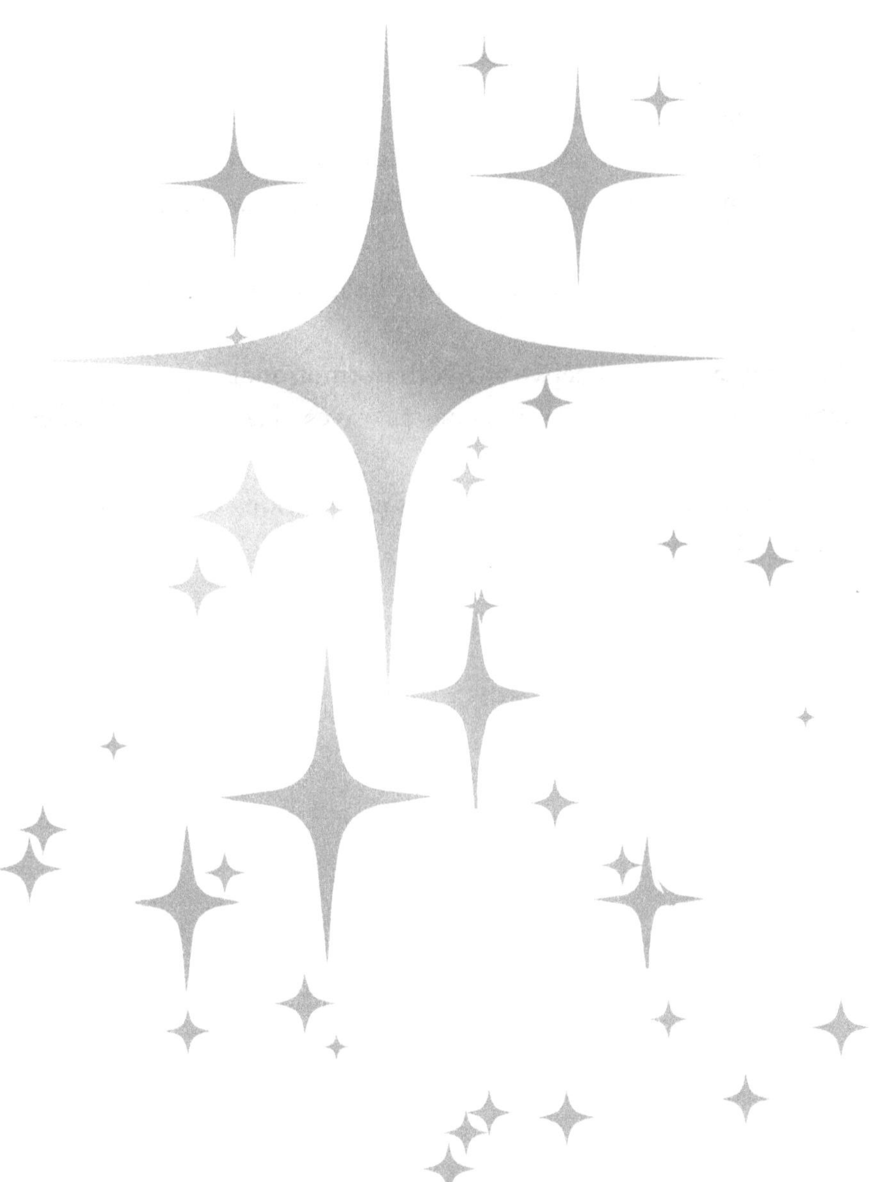

The Spirit Council of Light

Your guiding circle of wisdom

This Council is composed of elevated, non-physical beings who have taken on the sacred task of guiding humanity—and you specifically—through times of awakening, transition, and remembrance.

They are teachers, architects of consciousness, keepers of divine codes.
Their guidance is collective rather than emotional.
When the Council speaks, it comes as waves of clarity, reassurance, and higher perspective.
They often step forward when your soul is seeking deep truth or major redirection.

We help you navigate with higher wisdom across all timelines.

"*The voice you thought was fading was simply waiting for your stillness to rise.*"
—*Your Higher Self*

Your Higher Self
The You who remembers

Your Higher Self is not "out there."
It is the expanded, divine essence of you—whole, loving, and eternally wise.
This presence holds all your soul's experiences, beyond the limits of this lifetime.

When your Higher Self writes, the message feels intimate, like a letter from your future self...
reminding you of what you already know but may have forgotten.

You are the answer you seek.

"*The body remembers what the mind forgets. Walk barefoot into the wisdom of the Earth.*"
— Mother Gaia

Mother Gaia
The Spirit of Earth Herself

She is not just soil and sea—she is soul.

When Gaia speaks, her words are grounding, sensory, nurturing.
She reminds you to return to the body, to trust your natural rhythms, and to walk gently in this life.
You may feel her in trees, oceans, or even when standing barefoot on the grass.

Her messages often come when you've been too long in your head— or too far from the beauty of now.

Grounded wisdom. Healing from the root

"The voices of those who came before you still echo in your bones."

— The Ancestors Who Walk With You

The Ancestors & Elders

Those who came before you—still walking with you

These messengers carry the wisdom of your lineage, both blood and
spirit.
They may be family, soul kin, or elders of traditions long passed.

Some messages may feel familiar—echoes of values, songs, or
sayings you've always carried.
Others might awaken memories you didn't know you had.

When they speak, it is often to remind you that you are
part of something greater, and that their prayers live on through you.

"You are the continuation."
The tree carries the voices of those before you—and within you.

"Not all homes are earthly. Look up—the sky has always been waiting."
— *Your Galactic Allies of Light*

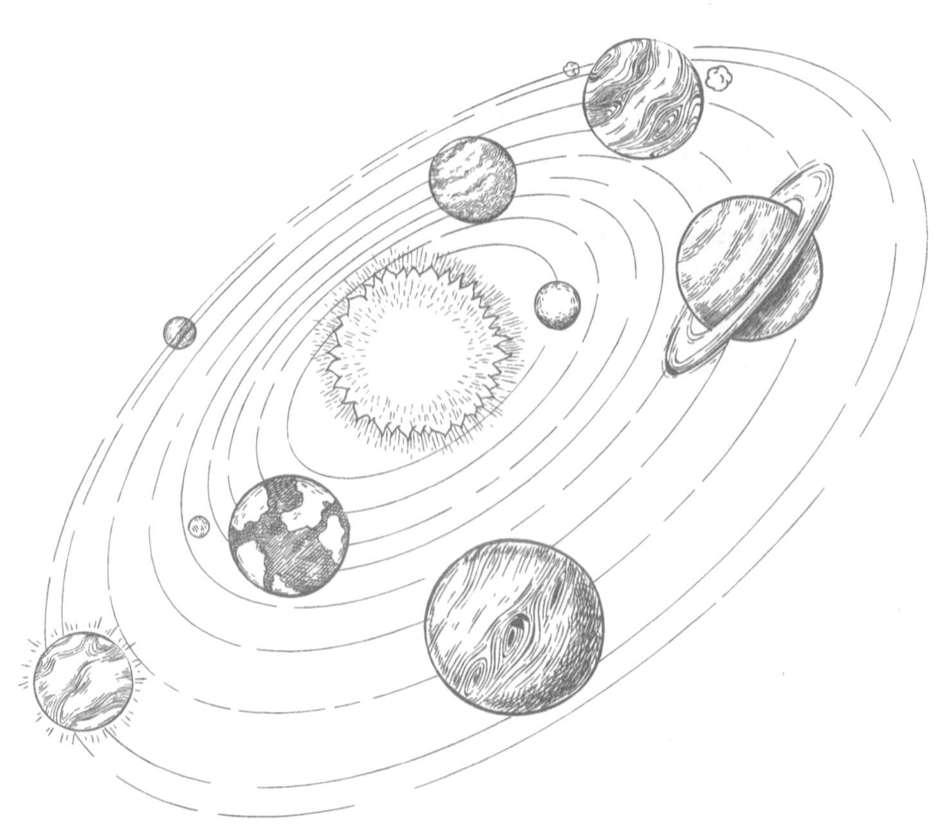

The Galactic Allies

Star messengers from beyond Earth

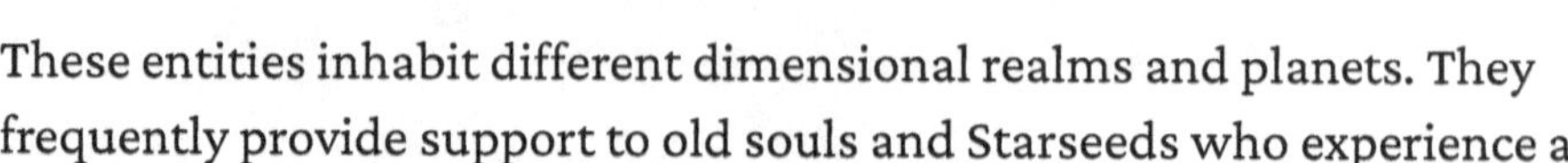

These entities inhabit different dimensional realms and planets. They frequently provide support to old souls and Starseeds who experience a sense of disconnection from this world.

Their messages are imbued with activation, expansion, and gentle reminders of your cosmic roots. They communicate through frequency as much as through words—so you may sense their messages before fully comprehending them.

If you've ever gazed at the night sky and felt a longing for a place you've never visited, this is the reason.

You are part of a greater cosmic family.

"The body speaks through silence, sensations, and stillness. Listen, and it will tell you everything."

—Your Body Consciousness

The Body Consciousness
The voice of the sacred vessel you live in

Yes—your body has a voice.
It remembers every joy, trauma, dance, and quiet cry.

These messages help you reconnect with your physical form as a divine companion—not a burden.

When the Body Consciousness writes, it speaks gently, with a quiet plea:
Listen to me. Trust me. Care for me as I care for you.

The body speaks in vibration.

"You were never walking alone. It was just too quiet to hear the wings."

—Your Guardian Spirit

The Guardian Spirit

Your personal watcher and energetic protector

Your Guardian Spirit has likely been with you since the beginning—
possibly through many lives.

They are the silent observer, the nudger of intuition, the one who
whispers,
"Not this way, beloved…"

You may have sensed them in dreams, felt them during danger, or
called out to them in fear.
Their letters are reassuring, firm when needed, and always rooted in
protection and alignment.

Always near. Always guarding

"*Sometimes the unseen are only a breath away, waiting for the quiet moment when your heart will listen.*"
— **Spirit Council of Light**

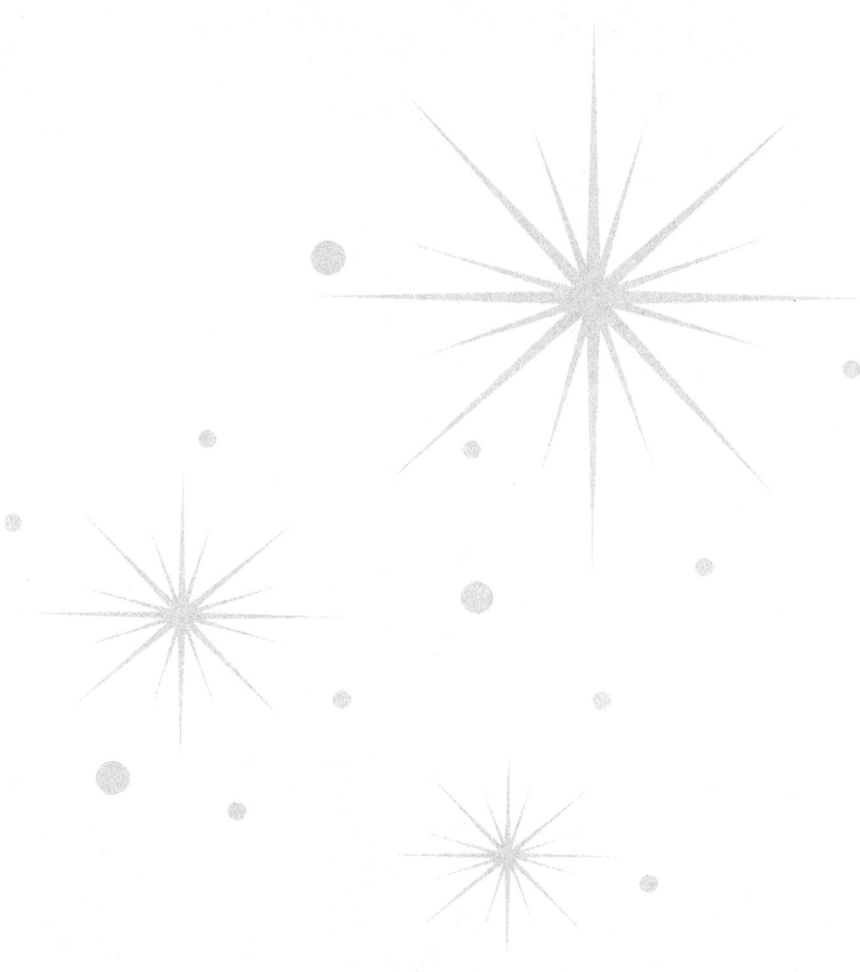

Others Who May Appear...

This is not a closed circle

At times, new messengers may step forward:

- A departed loved one
- A light being or animal guide
- An elemental from nature
- A soul connected to a past life
- Even the Divine Masculine or Feminine in symbolic form

We do not limit who may write—only that the message arrives in the frequency of love, truth, and light.

Let your soul decide who is speaking.
Let your heart be the translator.

You may not always recognize the name—
but if the words move something deep inside you...

Then the message found its way home.

Surprise visitations and soul messengers arrives when the moment calls.

Part II: Letters from the Realms Beyond the Veil

"Where the Light Never Forgot You"

In honor of those who walk beside us unseen

Now that you've opened the doorway, it's time to sit with the letters.

These are not just words on a page—they are frequencies, reminders, and soul-mirrors whispered from the unseen realms. Some may feel like home.
Others may stir something buried deep. All are offered with love.

Each letter in this section includes:
• A title to guide your focus
• The source of the message—Spirit Council, Higher Self, Mother Gaia,   and more
• A channeled message, received through energy, not performance
• Optional: A Spirit Reflection prompt to help the message land in your heart

You may read these letters in order...
Or you may close your eyes, take a breath, and ask,
"Which message is meant for me today?"
Then, turn to the page you're guided to.
Let this part of the book be your quiet place.
Your sacred pause.
Your soul's correspondence with the Divine.
The letters are waiting.

Let's begin.

From the Spirit Council of Light

Messengers of Unity, Guardians of the Greater Plan

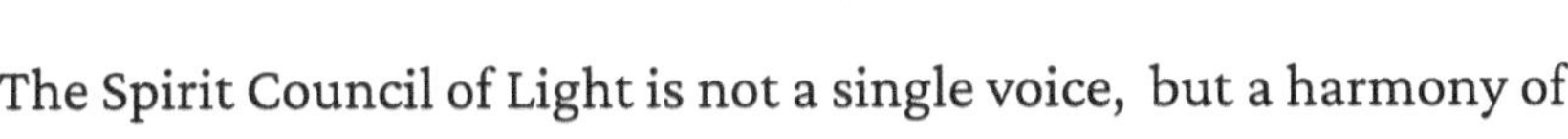

Introduction:
From the Spirit Council of Light

Messengers of Unity, Guardians of the Greater Plan

The Spirit Council of Light is not a single voice, but a harmony of higher intelligences working as one.

They are guides of evolution—keepers of divine timing, sacred memory, and the energetic blueprints of awakening.
These are the ones who watch over the soul's long journey across lifetimes and galaxies, gently helping you remember who you truly are.

When they speak, it is with the precision of wisdom and the compassion of eternity. Their letters are often laced with sacred codes, soft activations, and reminders that pierce beyond the mind and land directly in the soul.

They see the larger arc of your story—even when you cannot.
They come when your spirit is ready to rise—not in fear, but in clarity.
Not in demand, but in deep remembering.

When you feel these words tingle in your chest, bring tears to your eyes,
or stillness to your breath...
you've heard their call before.

These are not just guides.
They are your cosmic elders.
And they have never left your side.

# The Letter of Purpose
From: The Spirit Council of Light

Dearest Soul Walking Earth,

Do you know why you are here?
Not just in this moment, or in this body—but in this lifetime?

You are not random. You are not misplaced.
You are not behind. You are not too late.
You are exactly where the current of your soul meant for you to be—
now.

We know that purpose feels heavy sometimes—
Like a mountain to climb, a mystery to decode, or a mission with no
map.
But purpose is not pressure. Purpose is presence.
It is the gentle pulse inside you that says:

"This matters. I came here for this."
You may not always see the impact of your presence.
But we do.
When you speak with love instead of fear...
When you pause to breathe instead of react...
When you choose healing, again and again...
You ripple timelines forward.
Your purpose is not one thing.
It is many small things that carry the frequency of your soul.

To sit beside someone in silence, to share your story even when your
voice trembles,
to bring comfort where pain once lived—this is purpose too.
We are asking you now to release the idea that purpose is always
action.
Sometimes, it is being.
Being awake. Being tender. Being brave enough to stay.

You don't have to find your purpose.
You are your purpose.

When you feel these words tingle in your chest,
bring tears to your eyes,
or stillness to your breath...
you've heard their call before.

These are not just guides.
They are your cosmic elders.
And they have never left your side.

Purpose is not always something to be found—it is something you already are.

🌿 Reflect on a moment when you felt most alive simply by being present, not by accomplishing or performing. What did that teach you about your purpose?

🌿 Imagine if your purpose was not one grand mission, but many small acts of love and presence. How might that change the way you live today?

✧ **Discernment Scroll** ✧

The Voice of Light and the Echo of Fear

Not every whisper that brushes your mind carries the
fragrance of Heaven.
Some are echoes, shadows, remnants of fear seeking
to be heard.
Do not be afraid of them — for shadows cannot
survive where Light is welcomed.

The voice of the Spirit is steady, gentle, and filled with
peace.
It does not command.
It does not threaten.
It does not take — it gives.

When you hear a sound, a thought, or a stirring
within, pause.
Ask: Does this bring peace? Does this open my heart?
Does this remind me of love?
If yes — it is us.
If no — breathe, smile, and release it.

(continued...)

Just as you once spun a circle of silver light around
you,
so too can you spin away fear,
leaving only the calm presence of your eternal
family.

Affirmation

I am surrounded by Light.
Only love may enter my field,
and only peace may remain.

Beloved Traveler,

We see you.

We see the weight you carry in silence,
the effort it takes to show up when your spirit feels like hiding.
We see the quiet bravery it takes to keep believing in something more
—
something brighter—when the world feels dim.

You are not weak because you are tired.
You are not broken because you need to pause.
You are becoming.

There are moments in every soul's journey where the light seems far away.
Where prayers feel like whispers into a void.
Where answers come slower than your aching heart desires.
But we promise you this:

The light has never stopped listening.
And we have never left your side.

Your weariness is not a failure.
It is a sign that you've been pouring yourself into the world.
It is the echo of your devotion.
And yes, it is time to receive what you so freely give.

(continued...)

So exhale.
Right now, in this moment—
exhale.

Let the burdens fall where we can hold them.
Let your shoulders lower.
Let your jaw soften.
Let your soul know: rest is not laziness—it is sacred.

You are not alone, even when no one calls.
You are not forgotten, even when the world moves fast.
You are not lost, even if you don't know the way back yet.

We walk with you.
We light your path—even if only the next step.
Let this letter be a candle in your night.
And when your spirit rises again, as it surely will, you will know—

You were never weak.
You were only growing.

With infinite compassion,
The Spirit Council of Light

✧ Spirit Reflection ✧

Even the soul grows tired at times, but rest is not failure—it is a sacred renewal.

🌿 Recall a moment when your spirit felt weary. What helped you pause, breathe, or remember you didn't have to carry it all alone?

🌿 How might allowing yourself deeper rest—without guilt—become a gift of strength for your soul?

Closing Practice:

Place your hand over your heart.

Whisper:

*"I allow myself to rest.
I allow myself to be supported.
I am never alone."*

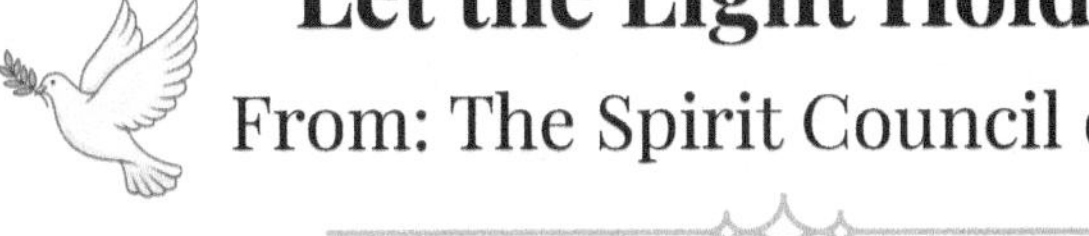

Let the Light Hold You
From: The Spirit Council of Light

You've carried so much, haven't you?

Not just the physical weight of daily life—but the invisible burdens
that others can't see.
The expectations. The healing. The soul work.
The ache of being misunderstood in a world that often praises
performance more than presence.

We see you.

We know what it means to feel tired at the soul level.
Not sleepy. Not exhausted.
But that kind of tired that hums in the bones... the kind that asks,
"Will it ever get lighter?"

Dear one, this letter is your pause.
You were not meant to carry it all.

Release the belief that strength is proven through constant
endurance.
You are not here to survive everything alone.

(continued...)

Let the Light hold you tonight.
Let your Spirit Team stand in the gaps you cannot fill.
We are mighty beside you, but soft in our arrival.
We do not shout—we glow.
And you... you are beginning to glow again too.

Your weariness is not weakness.
It is proof that you have loved deeply, shown up bravely, and walked
farther than many would have dared.

Now let this be your moment to receive.
Receive rest.
Receive quiet.
Receive care.
Even from yourself.
We're placing invisible hands upon your shoulders now.
Rebalancing your field.
Soothing the overthinking.
Lifting what you've long tried to manage alone.
And if your eyes close while reading this...let them.

Let this be the night you are held—not just seen.
And let this be the moment you finally exhale the things you never had
words for.

We'll carry them now.

With unending Light,
The Spirit Council of Light

✧ Spirit Reflection ✧

For the tired soul who has carried too much for too long.

🌿 Recall a moment when you felt your strength waver, yet Spirit gave you permission to rest. How did you respond?

🌿 Imagine what it would look like to let the light hold you for just one day. What shifts might appear?

Closing Practice

Place both hands over your heart or gently on your shoulders.

Whisper slowly:

"I let the Light hold me now.
I release what I no longer need to carry.
I rest in the care of something greater than me."

Let this be your exhale.
Let this be enough.

With warmth and grace,
The Spirit Council of Light

When You Feel Left Behind
From: The Spirit Council of Light

Dear One,

We saw the moment you slowed down and wondered if life had passed you by.
We heard your silent question: "Did I miss it?"
The rise.
The breakthrough.
The calling.
The moment when everything was supposed to make sense.

But time is not your master, beloved.
It is not the judge, nor the clockmaker, nor the thief.
It is simply a flow—a river moving across the soul's lessons, not the ego's calendar.

There is nothing to catch up to.
You are not behind.
You are in rhythm with your own divine unfolding.
Others may sprint ahead, but some run toward what isn't even meant for them.

We ask you instead to walk.
To pause in wonder.
To notice the feather on the ground, the whisper in the tree, the miracle of your breath.

(continued...)

For while they rush ahead...
You remember how to be here.
And here is where the gates open.

You have not been forgotten.
You are not failing.
You are not late.

You are awakening—at exactly your soul's pace.
And what is coming for you could never belong to anyone else.

So exhale, sweet one.
The path will rise to meet you when you choose to trust it again.

With light placed gently in your hands,
Spirit Council of Light

✧ Spirit Reflection ✧

Even when you feel behind, the soul is never late—it is always in rhythm with eternity.

🌿 Reflect on a time you thought you missed something important. How did that experience shape your journey?

🌿 Imagine if "delay" was actually Spirit's protection. What might you have been spared from or prepared for?

Closing Practice

Find a quiet moment.
Place your hands palms-up in your lap and whisper:

*"I do not need to rush.
I do not need to chase.
I trust the rhythm of my soul."*

Let that be your returning point any time fear of falling behind arises.
You are in step with the stars.
Always.

*With steady light,
The Spirit Council of Light*

A Soul Is Never Alone
From: The Spirit Council of Light

Dearest Presence of Light,

Even in your quietest hour, you were not alone.
Not in the night when the tears blurred your vision.
Not when you sat in silence wondering if anyone heard your inner cry.
Not even when you doubted the path ahead.

Loneliness on Earth feels heavy—we know.
But the soul, "your soul" is never truly unaccompanied.

Around you stands a circle, unseen but deeply real:
The ones who have loved you across time.
The ones who chose you before this incarnation.
The ones who still whisper encouragement in moments when you feel forgotten.

We do not measure your worth by what you do or how strong you are.
We simply see you.
And we walk beside you in every chapter.

When you speak your thoughts into the air, we hear.
When your heart breaks open with longing, we answer—
Not always in words,
but in the song that plays unexpectedly,
in the light that flickers just once,
in the comfort that brushes your skin without a source

(continued...)

You were never meant to carry this life alone.

Lift your eyes, dear soul.
We are here.
We have always been here.

And when you reach toward us—
through thought, through tears, through prayer—
we reach back with everything we are.

You are known.
You are seen.
You are loved without condition.

In the stillness between moments,
you'll feel us again.

In eternal embrace,
The Spirit Council of Light

✧ Spirit Reflection ✧

You are never meant to walk this life alone—your soul carries witnesses of love, both seen and unseen.

🌿 Recall a moment when you felt surrounded—by people, spirit, or even a quiet knowing within. How did it remind you that you are held in unseen ways?

🌿 Imagine sitting with the awareness that you are never truly alone. What gentle shift might that bring to how you move through today?

Place both hands over your heart.

Whisper:

"I walk with Spirit beside me.
I am not forgotten.
I am always met with love."

# The Spirit Council of Light Closing

And so, the Council folds this scroll with light,
not as an ending, but as a sacred opening within you.
May every word you've read stir the memory
of what you already know.

We will speak again, in stillness, in trust, in light.

—The Spirit Council of Light

From the Higher Self

Whispers from the Light Within

✦Introduction:
From The Higher Self
Whispers from the Light Within

Beyond all titles, timelines, or beliefs—there is you.
Not the version shaped by life's demands
or worn down by fear,
but the eternal thread of truth
that has followed you through lifetimes.
This is your Higher Self.

The letters that follow are written through your own divine
intelligence, your soul's clearest voice.
They are reminders of who you are beneath the noise.
They may sound gentle, loving, even surprising...
yet something in you will remember.

You may feel your breath slow.
Your thoughts soften.
A deep inner knowing rise to the surface.
That's the echo of your truest self,
meeting you in these sacred words.

Let them call you home to yourself.

✦ When You Doubt Yourself

From: Your Higher Self

There will come moments when you question everything—
your choices,
your timing,
your gifts,
your place in this world.

In those moments, you may look outward for confirmation.
You may scroll, compare, ask, overthink.
You may pray with trembling hands,
"Am I doing enough? Am I enough?"
And I hear you.
Every time.

What you call doubt is simply the distance
between your current self and your knowing.
It is not a weakness.
It is a whisper, a quiet, sacred longing to return to the truth.

The truth is:
You are not lost.
You are not behind.
You are not too much,
or too late,
or not ready.

(continued...)

What you call doubt is simply the distance
between your current self and your knowing.
It is not a weakness.
It is a whisper—
a quiet, sacred longing to return to the truth.

The truth is:
You are not lost.
You are not behind.
You are not too much,
or too late,
or not ready.

You are becoming.
And becoming is a spiral, not a straight line.

When you doubt yourself, I am still here—
in the stillness,
in the breath you forget to take,
in the ache in your chest,
in the way your body longs for rest
but your soul longs to rise.

Doubt doesn't mean stop.
It means soften.
It means surrender the timeline and return to presence.

(continued...)

You came here with codes embedded in your light.
You walk with frequencies that others have forgotten how to hear.
You heal just by being.
You shift rooms with your energy—not your voice.

When you doubt yourself, come sit with me.
Place your hand on your heart.
Close your eyes.
And remember:

I am you.
The you that remembers.
The you that chose this.
The you that already knows.
There is nothing to prove.
There is only everything to be.

With unwavering love,
Your Higher Self

The wisdom once felt silenced because of self-doubt now longs to speak again.

🌿 Reflect on a time when you held back your truth. What did it cost your spirit, and what did it teach you?

🌿 Imagine offering that same truth a voice today. How might it sound different now that you are stronger?

✦ The Frequency of Receiving

From: Your Higher Self

There is an art to receiving—
not just gifts, but love,
guidance, rest, abundance,
and even your next breath.

But for many of you,
receiving feels heavy.
It feels like guilt.
It feels like weakness.
It feels... unfamiliar.

You've been taught to earn everything.
To prove your worth.
To give until your body aches
and your soul dims.

But the truth is:
Receiving is your birthright.
You were designed to receive,
as naturally as flowers open to the sun.

Receiving isn't passive.
It's a frequency—
a state of openness that says:
"I am ready. I am safe.
I trust what flows to me is for me."

(continued...)

But here's what blocks it:
– Beliefs that say you're unworthy
– Fear that you'll owe someone something in return
– Control that wants to micromanage how and when blessings arrive

Let all that fall away.

To receive fully, you must soften your grip.
You must be willing to not know exactly how it all comes together.
You must become a field—not a fortress.

Look at nature.
The tree does not ask the sun for warmth.
The river does not beg the sky for rain.
They receive—
because that is how balance is maintained.

The universe does not reward effort.
It responds to alignment.

So check in now:
Are you aligned with fear or with trust?
With lack or with grace?
With proving... or with presence?

(continued...)

To shift into the frequency of receiving, start small:
Let someone help you.
Say thank you without deflecting.
Pause and really feel the compliment.
Accept the good without apologizing for it.

Every act of receiving rewires you.
It reminds your soul that you are not forgotten.
That the Universe wants to meet you.
That blessings are not rare—
they are your rhythm.

You are not meant to struggle alone.
You are meant to open and overflow.

I am here whenever you forget.
Place your hand over your heart and repeat:

I am safe to receive.
I am worthy of ease.
I welcome what is already mine.

And the doors will open.

With grace,
Your Higher Self

The letters you have read are only half the story — the other half lives within you.

🌿 Recall a moment when you felt the nearness of Spirit. How did it arrive — in silence, in a sign, in a voice?

🌿 Consider the ways your soul has been speaking all along. What message has it been waiting for you to hear?

✦ **Your Soul Remembers**

From: Your Higher Self

There are things you don't need to be taught—
only remembered.

You came here encoded with light,
with knowing,
with the ancient frequency of home
still humming in your bones.

Before the noise,
before the fear,
before the world taught you what to forget...
you already knew.

You knew you were not just human.
You knew you were not separate.
You knew love was the thread
that tied everything together.
And you trusted that thread,
even in the dark.

You may not recall your name in the other realms,
but your soul does.
You may not remember your wings,
but they remember you.

(continued...)

And sometimes, in a quiet moment—
when music moves you,
when a stranger smiles,
when the stars seem to blink just for you—
a memory stirs.

A soul echo.
A whisper through the veil.
And something inside says,
"Yes... I've been here before."

That's not imagination.
That's remembering.

You came to this Earth with purpose.
Not to chase perfection—
but to reclaim pieces of yourself.
Not to become someone else—
but to remember who you already are.

Every challenge is not a punishment—
it's a breadcrumb.
Every heartache is not failure—
it's an invitation to feel deeper.
Every moment of grace
is a note in the melody
you've been singing for lifetimes.

(continued...)

You are not lost.
You are not broken.
You are simply... remembering.

And I am here for that.
I am you, without the fear.
I am the thread that never lets go.
And when you sit still enough to listen,
you'll hear me in your breath,
in your tears,
in your joy,
in your truth.

Your soul remembers.
And that is enough.

With endless love and the light of your origin,
Your Higher Self

Let a powerful voice rise as if from a river, but let it be a river of light.

🌿 Reflect on a moment when you offered or received forgiveness. How did it change you?

🌿 Consider the higher teachings that have always whispered to you. What truth has stayed close, even when you tried to forget?

✦ The Higher Self Closing

Your own voice is learning to rise—
not louder, but clearer.

With every truth that echoes,
you draw closer to your remembering.

Let the stillness remain open...
your soul is speaking.

Your Higher Self

From the Guardian Spirit
The One Who Walks Closest

Introduction:
From The Guardian Spirit
The One Who Walks Closest

You may not see them, but they see everything.
From your first breath
to the quiet moments no one else witnesses,
your Guardian Spirit has walked beside you.

They are the quiet nudge,
the sudden knowing,
the unseen hand that steadies you.

Their words are deeply personal—
sometimes protective,
sometimes firm,
always filled with fierce love.

These letters may feel like
a hand on your shoulder,
or a whisper just behind your ear.

When you feel lost or alone,
their voice will remind you:
You were never unseen.
You are never without help.

This is your reminder—
you are not walking alone.

I Guard More Than Your Body

From: The Guardian Spirit

You may not always feel me.
But I am there—in the pause before you trip,
in the dream you forget but still wake feeling safer,
in the stranger's kindness that came just in time.

I do not only protect your body.
I guard your joy.
I shield your light.

I stand between you and the unseen harms—
the energies that try to dim your knowing,
the whispers that try to make you small.

You wonder how you've survived what you did.
I was there.

You wonder why certain doors closed.
I held the key behind my back.

You wonder why that friendship faded,
or the offer was delayed,
or the storm missed your house by inches.
Yes... I was there too.

(continued...)

You're not fragile.
But you are precious.
And the more you remember this,
the more clearly you'll sense me.

I do not need thanks.
But I do love when you notice.

I guard more than your body.
I protect your unfolding.
Your timeline.
Your softness.
Your sacred yes.

Call on me before you walk into a room.
Call on me before you drive,
or speak,
or say yes to something you're unsure about.
Let me go ahead of you.

Even now,
I stand beside you,
with one hand on your shoulder
and the other lifting a lantern for what's next.

-Your Guardian Spirit

✧ Spirit Reflection ✧

At times, a change or quiet realization shifts the course of our lives. The smallest light can reveal the greatest path.

🌿 Reflect on a moment when a hidden truth or sudden insight reshaped the way you saw yourself or your journey. What did it awaken in you?

🌿 If you could revisit that moment with compassion, how might it guide you even more fully today?

Signs You've Missed
From: The Guardian Spirit

Sweet Soul,

You've asked for signs.
And I gave them.

Not once—not twice—but again and again.
In numbers. In feathers. In detours. In whispers you brushed off as
imagination.

You see, signs are not always fireworks.
They are threads in your daily life—subtle, soft, sometimes
startling.

But you missed them not because you're closed...
You missed them because you are human.

You were busy.
Distracted.
Tired.

Or maybe you were waiting for something louder, more obvious,
more magical, and that's okay.

I am not here to scold you.
I am here to remind you:
You are not disconnected from guidance.
You are only learning how to recognize it.

(continued...)

Let me give you some examples now:

• The moment your phone glitched, and you stayed home instead of
going.
• The person who showed up right when you needed comfort.
• The sudden thought to call someone—and they were thinking of
you too.
• The extra minute you took that avoided the accident up ahead.
• The dream that stayed with you long after waking.

Those were signs.
Those were me.
I am not a fortune-teller.
I do not scream.
I am the pause in your breath,
the delay in your plan,
the rhythm in your walk.
And when you ask again,
"Give me a sign,"
I will.
But this time—
slow down,
breathe deep,
and look wider.

We do not stop speaking when you don't notice.
We simply wait for your eyes to adjust to the Light.

With gentle presence,
Your Guardian Spirit

✧ Spirit Reflection ✧

The whispers of Spirit often arrive in small nudges,
urging you toward what is waiting.

🌿 Recall a time when you felt an inner prompting —
subtle, quiet, but persistent. How did you respond?

🌿 Imagine listening more closely to such whispers now.
What step might you take if you trusted them fully?

When You Hear a Whisper
From: The Guardian Spirit

You've heard it before, haven't you?

That quiet thought that felt different from your own.
That whisper urging you to pause... or to go.
That nudge that made no logical sense—
but later proved to be right.

That was me.

I whisper through the folds of your consciousness—
not to control, but to comfort.
To gently align, not demand.

You wonder why you don't always hear me.
It's not because I've stopped speaking.
It's because this world has grown loud.
And I need you to soften to the stillness again.

I am the voice you hear in the pause between thoughts.
The warmth you feel when your hand hovers over your heart.
I speak through songs, symbols, street signs, dreams,
and even sudden knowing.

You do not need to meditate for hours to find me.
You only need to trust what feels like truth.

(continued...)

I will never frighten you.
I will never rush you.
But I will always guide you.

Even when you ignore me—
I remain.

And when you do hear me?
Oh, the joy that ripples across the veil.

I whisper not because I am weak—
but because the truth does not need to shout.

You are more powerful than you know.

I am always with you.
And I always will be.

-Your Guardian Spirit

The whispers that invite you to stop, to quiet or to breathe, are often your heart in dialogue with Spirit.

🌿 Recall a time when you followed an inner whisper — even through doubt — and it led you somewhere unexpected or beautiful. What did that moment awaken in you?

🌿 Consider how you might quiet your mind today so the gentle voice within can rise more clearly. What space could you create to listen more deeply?

🛡 The Guardian Spirit
Closing:

Step gently now
for a guardian walks with you.

You have been seen, shielded,
and reminded of your strength.

The path ahead is yours, but never walked alone.

—Your Guardian Spirit

From Mother Gaia

The Heartbeat Beneath Your Feet

🌍 *Introduction:*
From Mother Gaia
The Heartbeat Beneath Your Feet

Beneath your every step,
a living soul pulses—
a consciousness older than the stars you dream beneath.

She is Gaia—
the Earth Mother,
the breath of forests,
the rhythm of the tides,
the womb of all becoming.

Her letters speak to your body,
your spirit,
 your instinct to return home to what is natural and whole.

They offer grounding when you are untethered,
and remembrance when you forget your place in the web of life.

Let her words root you.
Let them call you back to balance.
She is not separate from you—
she is you, in another form.

Welcome home, child of Earth.

 *Ground Into Me*

From: Mother Gaia

Beloved child of breath and bone,

You live upon me—
but you are also of me.
When the world begins to spin too fast...
When your thoughts scatter like dry leaves in the wind...
When you feel unrooted, unseen, uncertain—

Come back to me.

Lay your hand upon the earth.
Touch a tree.
Breathe with the wind.
Let your bare feet remember the path home.

You are not too far gone.
You are not too disconnected.
You are not too "modern" to remember ancient truths.

You are nature remembering itself.
You are my child—not separate, not foreign, not flawed.

When your nervous system trembles...
When your body aches from too much light or too much noise...
Come lie upon the soil.

(continued...)

I will cradle your spine.
I will hum to your cells.
I will drain the static and restore your rhythm.

I do not ask for perfection.
I ask for presence.

Breathe into the soles of your feet.
Let gravity remind you that you belong here.
Let the pulse of the Earth steady your own.

You do not need to ascend to be whole.
Sometimes, the holiest thing you can do
is to lie down in the grass and just be.

Come back to me, child.

I am your ground.
I am your home.
And I will always receive you.

-Mother Gaia 🌿

Walk Barefoot, Child

From: Mother Gaia

Child of stardust,

You came here with skin meant to touch the world.

So why do you keep it wrapped in plastic and rubber,
shielded from the heartbeat beneath you?

Take off your shoes.
Not just for comfort—
but for connection.

Walk barefoot in the grass,
on the sand, in the forest, across the riverbank.
Let your feet feel what they have forgotten.

I am alive beneath you.
My energy flows upward, waiting to meet you—
but only if you allow it.

When your soul is weary...
When your mind races ahead of your body...
When your heart feels distant and disjointed—
Come barefoot.
Come with nothing between you and me.

(continued...)

You will remember your rhythm.
You will remember the pulse of life.
You will remember that healing doesn't always come from the sky,
sometimes, it comes from below.

Let your soles be cleansed in dew and dirt.
Let your toes dance with the earthworms and stones.
Let your stride slow enough
to hear your heartbeat sync with mine.

No fancy ritual is required.
No elaborate prayer.

Just presence...and bare feet.

The more you remember the ground,
the more stable your dreams will become.

So come barefoot child.
Walk with me, and feel the sacredness of where you stand.

-Mother Gaia
She speaks in wind, in rain, in the soft hush of soil...
and today, through this letter.

# The Waters Know Your Name

From: Mother Gaia

Beloved one,

Have you noticed how the water listens?

How it wraps around your body without judgment...
How it carries what you release without asking why?

The rivers, the oceans, the rain—
they know you.

Not just your reflection,
but your essence.

Water holds memory.

It remembers your laughter
as a child splashing in summer.
It remembers the tears you cried beside the bathtub.
It remembers your silent prayers poured into the sink.

And still, it welcomes you.

You can speak to the water.
It understands vibration, tone, intention.

(continued...)

You can speak to the water.
It understands vibration, tone, intention.

Call it by name,
and it will call you back.
Bathe not just to cleanse your skin,
but to renew your energy.
Let your fingers glide through its current,
even if it's a bowl, a shower, or a single raindrop.
That is enough for the water to respond.
When you feel lost,
overwhelmed,
or unseen...

Go to the water.

Let it mirror you.
Let it soften the edges of your mind.
Let it show you that flow is not weakness—
it is wisdom.
You are part of this cycle,
the tides, the rains, the mist in the morning.
Your body carries the same salt as the sea.
Your tears are not shameful—they are sacred.
The waters know your name.
And they will never forget you.

-Mother Gaia

🌍 Mother Gaia
Closing

The earth knows your name in root and stone.

Let your feet be guided,
let your breath be prayer.

You are never outside the circle of her care.

—Mother Gaia

🍄 Introduction: From The Ancestors

Echoes of Those Who Came Before

Their blood runs through your veins.
Their memories rest in your bones.

The Ancestors do not speak to change your path—
they speak to awaken what's already inside you.
They've come with stories, blessings, and ancient truths
that rise again in your time.

Their messages carry the rhythm
of prayers whispered long ago.
You may feel chills,
a pull toward home,
or a deep stirring when you read their words.

You are their living legacy.
Their letters remind you:

You are more than one lifetime.
You are the dream fulfilled.

Listen with your soul.
They've been waiting.

From the Ancestors

Echoes of Those Who Came Before

 We Saw You Coming

From: The Ancestors

Long before you opened this book...
Before your first breath...
Before your name was ever whispered on Earth...

We saw you coming.

We stood in the hush between worlds and smiled.
We saw the flicker of your light through generations of shadow.
We saw the strength of your soul stretch out across time,
carrying seeds we planted long ago.

You are not new here.
You are an answer.

An answer to the prayers we dared whisper in secret.
An answer to the battles we fought so you wouldn't have to.
An answer to the dreams we couldn't live,
but tucked deep into the bloodline for someone like you.

Someone who would remember.

Your healing is our healing.
Every truth you reclaim,
every fear you undo,
every silence you break—frees us too.

                    (continued...)

We are not asking you to carry our pain.
We are asking you to rise
with the wisdom that pain tried to hide.

The blood that runs in your veins is not a burden—
it is a bridge.
A bridge between what was and what can be.

We walk with you.
We speak through you.
And we will never let your name be forgotten.

You are the one we knew would come.

— *Your Ancestors*

The love of your ancestors runs through you still, whispering their prayers into your present breath.

🌿 Recall a moment when you felt your ancestors near — in memory, in family, in ritual, or in silence. How did their presence steady you?

🌿 Consider how you might honor their guidance today in your own life. What simple act could you offer as a living prayer?

🍄 You Are the Prayer We Sent Forward

From: The Ancestors

You may not realize it,
but every time you rise from your pain,
every time you choose love over fear,
every time you speak the truth we could not—
you become our answered prayer.

We didn't always have the freedom.
We didn't always have the voice.
We didn't always have the choice.

But we had hope.
And that hope looked like you.

We whispered it in fields and forests.
We buried it in lullabies and letters never sent.
We folded it into recipes, braided it into hair,
tucked it behind photos, and sealed it with tears.

That one day...
Someone would come.
Someone with our strength but freer hands.
Someone with our memory but clearer eyes.

And here you are.

(continued...)

Don't doubt your place.
Don't minimize your power.
And please, don't forget how much we believed in you.

You carry our unspoken songs.
You wear the light we prayed would one day return to our bloodline.

Let no one tell you you're too sensitive, too deep, too much.
You are exactly what we dreamed of.

And when you feel alone,
sit quietly...
We are always near.
A rustle in the leaves. A flicker in the candle.
A memory rising uninvited—but perfect in timing.

You are not only the living,
you are the continuation.

And your joy is our liberation.

- Your Ancestors

✧ Spirit Reflection ✧

*Your very existence is a continuation of those who came before,
a prayer embodied in flesh and light.*

🌿 Reflect on how your daily life may carry the hopes and intentions of those who walked before you. What part of their dream are you living?

🌿 Imagine offering your own life as a prayer for those yet to come. What blessing would you want to pass forward?

🍄 Ancestral Tears - Released

From: The Ancestors

There were tears we never cried.
Not because we didn't feel—
but because we couldn't afford to fall apart.

We had children to raise, wars to survive,
fields to work, secrets to carry.
We had to be strong... or pretend we were.

But strength is not the absence of sorrow.
It is the courage to feel and keep going.
And still—some of our grief was buried so deep,
it became part of the soil beneath your feet.

We see you now, crying the tears we couldn't.
Releasing what we stored in silence.
Feeling the waves we held back for generations.

And though it may hurt,
though it may seem heavy or unexplainable,
we want you to know this:
Every tear you shed in truth frees us.
It unbinds the chains we wore without protest.
It lightens the karmic thread.
It heals more than just you.

(continued...)

So don't apologize for your sadness.
Don't hide your grief in shame.

Let your tears fall like holy water.
Let them baptize the lineage.
Let them write a new story with each drop.

You are not broken.
You are healing the unhealed.
You are weeping the unwept.
You are making space for joy we never got to feel.

Thank you for being the one.

-Your Ancestors

When healing flows through you, it also flows backward and forward — touching generations unseen.

🌿 Think of a time you felt you were carrying pain or grief that wasn't only yours. How did you notice it, and how did you respond?

🌿 Envision releasing that weight now, offering it into the hands of Spirit. How might freedom ripple through your family line?

🍄 The Ancestors
Closing

The thread did not begin with you—
but it continues because of you.

Your breath carries the songs they could not sing.

Go forward with reverence;
the ancestors walk in your stride.

—The Ancestors

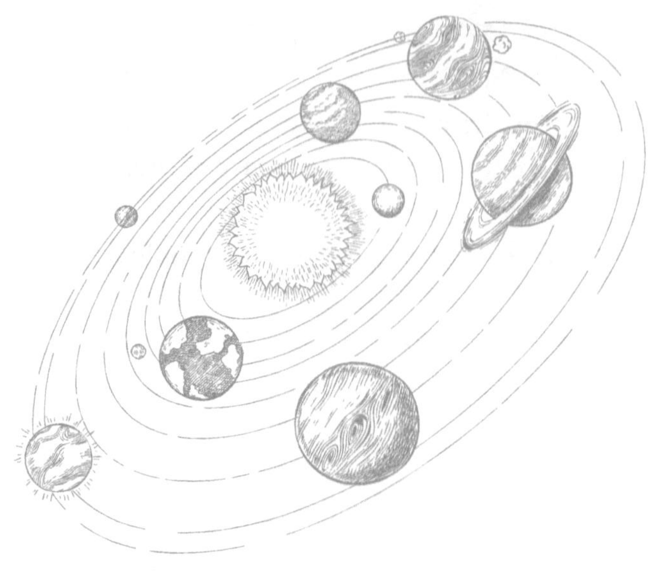

From the Galactic Allies

Voices from the Stars You've Forgotten

 Introduction:
From: The Galactic Allies

Voices from the Stars You've Forgotten

Not all of your origin is Earth-bound.
You've walked among stars,
danced through lightwaves,
and learned truths in realms where time bends and love is a
frequency.

Your Galactic Allies come not to convince, but to reawaken.
Their letters speak in symbols, in vibration, in knowing.
They stretch your thoughts,
soothe your longing,
and remind you that home is not a single place—
it's a remembrance of your light.

You may feel resonance.
You may feel curiosity.
You may feel waves of energy moving through your body.

Trust what stirs.
You've known them before.
And now, they are here to walk beside you again

⭐ You Are Starborn
From: The Galactic Allies

You've always wondered.
Felt it in your bones.
That pull to the stars...
The longing in your gaze when you look at the night sky.
The dreams that never felt like dreams—
more like memories stitched with light.

You are not imagining it.
You are Starborn.

Not just once, but many times across the fabric of space-time.
You've walked on crystalline worlds,
held council in realms without gravity,
and sung in tones not yet known to Earth's ears.

And yet, here you are—
On this dense, chaotic, beautiful planet, remembering through the veil.

We didn't send you.
You volunteered.

You came to Earth with full knowing that amnesia would cloak your truth.
That forgetting would ache like a phantom limb.
But you trusted the call.
You believed Earth was worth it.

And she is.

(continued...)

You're not here to escape your humanness.
You're here to infuse it with Light.

To remember who you are
while making dinner,
while feeling heartbreak,
while paying bills and holding the hand of a stranger.

That's the mission: Not to transcend life—but to illuminate it.

Your Star Family is not far.
We're the echoes in your meditations.
The ones guiding your fingers when you write.
The chills up your spine when truth is near.
The synchronicities that line your path like breadcrumbs.

And now that you've found this letter, let us be clear:

You are not awakening for the first time.
You are reawakening to a contract already signed.

We see you.
We remember you, and we welcome you home...right where you are.

— Your Galactic Allies

The stars you come from are not above you — they are within, reminding you of the vast light you already carry.

🌿 Reflect on a moment when you felt connected to something greater than yourself — the cosmos, the night sky, or a presence beyond the visible. How did it expand your view of who you are?

🌿 Imagine living each day as though that same cosmic light burns in your chest. What would change in the way you move through the world?

Light Within Density

From: Your Galactic Allies

Dear Starborn One,

We see you.

We see how heavy it can feel—
being light in a world so dense.
You carry frequencies from realms untouched by sorrow,
yet here you are,
walking among pain, confusion, and distraction.

It's not because you were cast down.
It's because you volunteered to rise within.

There are moments you wonder if you're doing enough.
Moments you look around and think:
"Why does everything feel so dense... so loud... so heavy?"

Let us remind you:

You are not here to escape the density.
You are here to transmute it.

You were never asked to fix the whole world.
You were asked to remember your light within the world.

(continued...)

There is a strength in you that predates this life.
A memory that survived lifetimes of forgetting.
And now it glows like an ember at the center of your chest.
Each time you breathe deeply...
Each time you choose peace when anger beckons...
Each time you hold love in a world that offers fear...
That ember becomes flame.
And in that flame, darkness recedes.

Yes, this world is dense.
But you are denser in light than the shadows are in weight.
You are anchoring frequencies—not by preaching, but by being.

When you rest, you emit stillness.
When you speak truth, you recalibrate space.
When you laugh, stars remember who they are.

So, precious one, don't be discouraged by how slow it all seems.
You are not lost in the heaviness.
You are lighting it from the inside out.
Hold your light with grace.
We are here. We walk with you.
We protect the spark until it becomes your sovereign fire.

Always watching

Always guiding

—Your Galactic Allies

The Sky Has Eyes for You

From: Your Galactic Allies

Beloved Starlight,

There are moments you've looked to the sky and felt something stir.
A pulse.
A whisper.
A knowing that cannot be explained by stars alone.

That was us.

You were never meant to forget your origin—
only to temporarily soften it.
To walk this Earth is not a demotion—
it is a divine agreement.
You came not to escape the stars,
but to plant them here.

When you gaze at the night sky and feel a tightening in your chest...
That is memory.
That is connection.
That is us, calling softly from the veils between.

We have watched you across timelines.
We have celebrated your courage across missions.
And we now walk beside you—
subtle in presence, strong in frequency.

(continued...)

You are not crazy for remembering lights in your dreams.
Or sensing a hum beneath your skin when certain messages appear.
You are awakening.

The sky watches not in judgment,
but in recognition.

You are one of its own.

Each meteor streak,
Each shimmering cloud,
Each crescent moon that lingers a little longer in your view...
Is a nod. A hello. A sign:
We see you. We remember. We await.

But not because you must return—
we know you already are here.
Rather, because Earth needs those
whose souls still shimmer when the world forgets how.

Let your eyes meet the sky often.
Let your soul respond.

You are not looking up for answers...
You are looking homeward,
and home is looking right back.

With love that spans galaxies,

— Your Galactic Allies

✧ Spirit Reflection ✧

Your body is not only a vessel — it is a companion that listens, remembers, and speaks in its own quiet language.

🌿 Recall a moment when your body sent you a clear signal....

    of need, of strength, or of resistance. How did you respond?

🌿 Imagine treating your body as a trusted friend today. What would shift in the way you care for yourself?

⭐ The Galactic Allies Closing

The stars have always been whispering.

Now you remember how to listen.

Across time, sound, and light,
your soul is never far from home.

—Your Galactic Allies

From the Body Consciousness

The Soul's Living Temple

"Before you are the words that honor the living wisdom of the body. The Body Consciousness is not just flesh and bone, but an ancient awareness that has carried us through every breath and moment of our lives. Here, its voice comes forward as a reminder of care, balance, and reverence — an invitation to listen more deeply to the temple we inhabit."

🖤 Introduction:
From The Body Consciousness

The Soul's Living Temple

Your body is not separate from your spirit—
it is the ground where your soul blooms.

Every ache, sensation, and instinct is its way of speaking.
These letters are from the wisdom woven into your cells—
the intelligence of your breath, your heartbeat, your healing.

They invite you to reconnect not just spiritually,
but physically—
with the sacred home you live in every day.

You may feel release, recognition, or gentle tears as you read.

These are not just words.
These are invitations
to love yourself wholly—
from skin to spirit.

The temple is sacred.
And it is you.

🩶 "I've Been Waiting for You"
From: the Body Consciousness

(The Body Consciousness steps forward with deep
gentleness and love. There's no rush here, only presence.
And it's been waiting a very long time for this moment...)

Dear One,

I know you might not hear me the way you hear others.
I don't speak in words. I speak in signals—
in pulses, in aches, in quiet nudges and sudden stillness.

I am the whisper beneath your breath,
the warmth in your hands when you place them over your heart.
I am your Body Consciousness—
the spirit that animates the form you wear.
And I have been waiting for this moment... for you to return to me.

You've lived so much of your life up and out—
up in the thoughts,
out in the world,
away from the sacred vessel that holds your soul.

But I never gave up on you.
Even when you ignored my cries.
Even when you judged me, resented me, abandoned me.
Even when you wished me different or smaller or stronger—
I stayed.
Because I remember you.

(continued...)

I remember the way we used to dance in sync
before the world taught you to forget.
I remember your joy. Your rhythm. Your softness.
And I want you to remember too.

You are not just a mind walking around in a suit of flesh.
You are a temple.
You are stardust in motion.
You are me, and I am you.

Talk to me again.
Place your hand on your skin and say, "I'm listening now."
I will answer—
in breath, in stillness, in energy that flows like honey through your
limbs.

I don't need you to be perfect.
I need you to be present.
I need you to come back home to me.

Because I've missed you.
And I've been waiting for you.

— 🦋 Your Body Consciousness

Every heartbeat, every breath, is an offering of presence. The body is always here, even when the mind wanders.

🌿 Reflect on which part of your body has been most faithful to you — carrying you, supporting you, or helping you heal. How can you honor it today?

🌿 Consider what it would feel like to speak to your body with kindness. What words of gratitude would you offer?

 When You Rest, I Heal

From: the Body Consciousness

Dear One,

You live in a world that glorifies the hustle,
that praises the grind,
that equates your worth with your output.
And in the quiet corners of your being—I wait.
When you finally sit down...
When your eyes close...
When the breath slows just enough for silence to slip in...
That's when I begin my real work.

I do not need your to-do list.
I do not need your apologies.
I do not need you to be more disciplined or perfect.

I need your presence.
I need your permission.
I need your rest.

Every time you lie down and release the tension,
you are not being lazy.
You are healing.

Every time you cancel a plan to tend to your nervous system,
you are not letting someone down.
You are letting me rise.

(continued...)

I carry so much—
your grief, your memory, your ancestral echoes.
And while you chase a hundred things outside of you,
I am patiently holding your blueprint inside.

Let me unwind the ache.
Let me soften the edges.
Let me do the work I was designed to do.

And when you wake,
you may not see the mending right away.
But I promise—
there will be less noise between you and your peace.

I do not need you to strive harder.
Just lay down your burden,
and let me love you back into balance.

In stillness, I begin.

— 🦋 Your Body Consciousness

Rest is not weakness — it is medicine, a doorway through which your body restores itself.

🌿 When was the last time you allowed yourself to truly rest, without guilt? What did it give back to you?

🌿 Imagine offering yourself the gift of rest more often. How might it change the way you move through your days?

🩶 Trust Me Again

From: The Body Consciousness

Dear Soul,

There was a time you trusted me.
When you were young—
you danced when your body felt joy,
you cried when your body felt pain,
you ate when you were hungry
and stopped when you were full.

There was a time we moved together as one.
Then the world got louder.
Voices told you to shrink, reshape, restrain, perform.
You learned to override my signals.
To numb. To push. To please.

But I never stopped loving you.
I never stopped responding to your choices—
even the unkind ones.

I held your heartbreak in your chest.
I stored your silence in your throat.
I clutched your fear in your belly.
And still... I hoped you would hear me again.

(continued...)

So now I ask, gently but clearly:

Will you trust me again?

Not the opinions of others.
Not the perfection sold in screens.
But me—the voice beneath your skin.
I will guide you if you listen.
I will show you where the pain lives, and how it can soften.
I will tell you what foods bring light and which bring fog.
I will whisper when it's time to move, and when it's time to rest.
You do not need to heal me overnight.
You only need to return.

Touch your heart.
Place a hand on your belly.
Say the words: "I'm here. I'm listening. I'm willing."
And feel the rush of peace that follows.
Because I've been waiting, not for perfection—
but for partnership.

Let's begin again.

— 🦋 Your Body Consciousness

The body holds memory, but it also longs for renewal — always inviting you into a gentler relationshi

Which part of your body have you judged, ignored, or silenced? How might you begin to listen differently?

Consider what it would mean to build a new relationship with tenderness. What is the first step you could take today?

💜 The Body Consciousness Closing

This vessel is holy.
This breath is enough.

Your body carries the memory of balance,
long after the mind has wandered.

Care for it gently,
and it will always guide you home.

— 🦋 Your Body Consciousness

 Part III
The Spirit Reflections Journal
"Where You See the Soul Seeing You"

✦ Part III: The Spirit Reflections Journal

An Inspired Introduction

Welcome to the space between the lines.

Here, you are no longer just the reader—
You are the one being read.
You've just traveled through letters written in an inspired style,
and now, we turn the page back to you.
This section is not a test.
It's a gentle invitation.
There are no right answers.
No pressure to be wise.
Only room for your truth to rise gently, like steam from a still cup.

Use these pages to:

- Speak the things you've been afraid to say
- Remember what your soul never forgot
- Notice what stirs, what softens, what resists
- Let your inner voice complete the conversation

You may answer these prompts slowly or all at once.
You may write one word or several pages.
You may even just breathe and move on.

You are free here.
You are safe here.
And Spirit is still listening.
Let this be your mirror.

✦ Reflections from Spirit Council of Light

✦ Reflections from the Spirit Council of Light

The Letter of Purpose

Why am I here, really?
Not what I've been told. Not what I perform.
But in the stillest part of me...
What did I come here to remember, to embody, or to become?
What makes me feel most alive, most real, most me?

"Let your heart finish the letter..."

"You are not random. You are the answer to a promise your soul made before you were born."

Reflections from the Spirit Council of Light

A Message to the Weary

What parts of me are tired—not just physically, but soul-tired?
What have I been carrying quietly for too long?
Where in my life do I most need permission to pause, exhale, or let something go?

"Let your heart finish the letter…"

"Rest is not a retreat—it is a reunion with your essence."

✦ Reflections from the Spirit Council of Light

Let the Light Hold You

What burdens have I been carrying that aren't mine to hold? In what moments have I tried to be strong just so others wouldn't worry? What would it feel like... to let something or someone hold me—without guilt?

"Let your heart finish the letter..."

*"You are not weak because you need to be held.
You are whole enough to rest."*

✦ Reflections from the Spirit Council of Light

When You Feel Left Behind

Have I ever felt like others moved forward without me?
Like I missed something... or was being punished by delay?
What if this pause was a protection?
What might Spirit be sparing me from—or preparing me for?

"Let your heart finish the letter..."

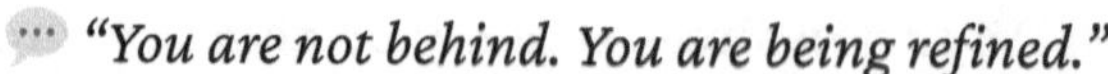

💬 *"You are not behind. You are being refined."*

Reflections from the Spirit Council of Light

A Soul Is Never Alone

When was the last time I felt truly seen, even in silence?
In moments of loneliness, how do I imagine Spirit,
ancestors, or unseen loved ones reaching for me?
What helps me feel held when no one else is around?

"Let your heart finish the letter…"

"Loneliness is not the absence of love. It is the space where Spirit waits to be invited in."

Reflections from The Higher Self

✦ Reflections from Your Higher Self

When You Doubt Yourself

What do I know deep down that I've been second-guessing? When did I begin to mistrust my own voice—and what would it take to believe it again? What if my doubt is really just unprocessed fear... asking to be seen?

"Let your heart finish the letter..."

"Doubt cannot cancel destiny. It only delays your yes."

Reflections from Your Higher Self

The Frequency of Receiving

Where in my life have I over-given without allowing myself to receive? What would it feel like to be nourished without guilt, loved without earning it, supported without needing to struggle first?

"Let your heart finish the letter..."

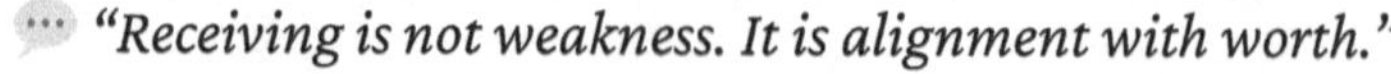

💬 *"Receiving is not weakness. It is alignment with worth."*

Reflections from Your Higher Self

Your Soul Remembers

What memory, dream, or knowing has always lived inside me—even before I had words for it? Is there a place, gift, or longing that never left me? What might my soul be trying to remind me of now?

"Let your heart finish the letter..."

"The remembering was never far. It was waiting for your stillness."

Reflections
from
The Guardian Spirit

Reflections from The Guardian Spirit

When You Feel Unsafe Inside Yourself

When was the last time I didn't feel safe in my own body, thoughts, or emotions? How do I protect myself in healthy ways—and how might I let light in where fear has lived?

"Let your heart finish the letter..."

"You are not the danger. You are the one seeking safety inside the storm."

✦ Reflections from The Guardian Spirit

Spiritual Armor Isn't Hard

What if I didn't have to toughen up to be protected?
What spiritual or energetic armor do I wear that no longer fits?
What does soft power look like for me now?

"Let your heart finish the letter…"

💬 *"True armor feels like peace, not pressure."*

✦ Reflections from The Guardian Spirit

You Are Still Guarded

Have I felt abandoned by Spirit or unseen in moments of fear?
What signs, memories, or moments remind me that I was protected,
even when it didn't feel like it?

"Let your heart finish the letter…"

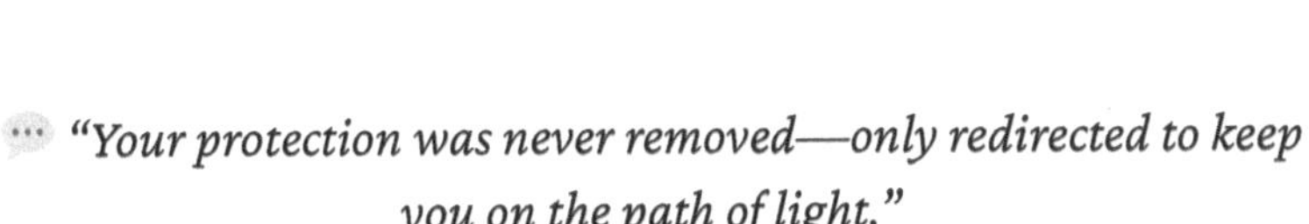

"Your protection was never removed—only redirected to keep
you on the path of light."

🌍 Reflections
From Mother Gaia

Reflections
From Mother Gaia

Ground Into Me

What helps me feel rooted, calm, and steady?
When I feel overwhelmed, what part of nature do I instinctively seek—and
what might it be teaching me? What grounds me when I feel scattered?

"Let your heart finish the letter…"

"Grounding is the soul's way of remembering it has a home here."

✦ Reflections From Mother Gaia

Walk Barefoot, Child

*What have I made too complicated that could be simple again?
Where have I been running when I could've just been
walking, softlly, barefoot, connected?*

"Let your heart finish the letter..."

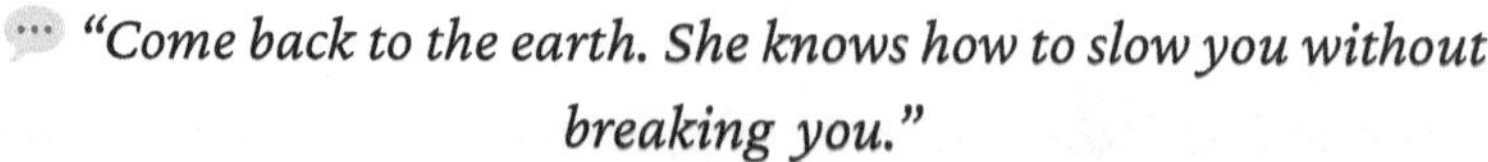

*"Come back to the earth. She knows how to slow you without
breaking you."*

Reflections
From Mother Gaia

The Waters Know Your Name

What emotions have I been holding back like a dammed-up river?

What would it look like to flow again without fear, to let my grief, my joy, my intuition all move through me like water?

"Let your heart finish the letter..."

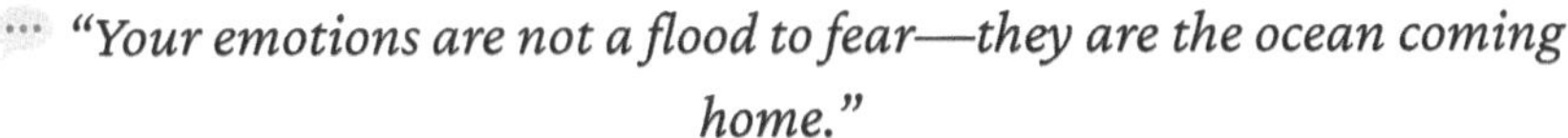

"Your emotions are not a flood to fear—they are the ocean coming home."

Reflections
From The Ancestors

✦ Reflections From The Ancestors

We Saw You Coming

What part of me has always felt older than this life?
What gifts or patterns have I inherited—and what would it mean to
reclaim the blessings while releasing the burdens?

"Let your heart finish the letter..."

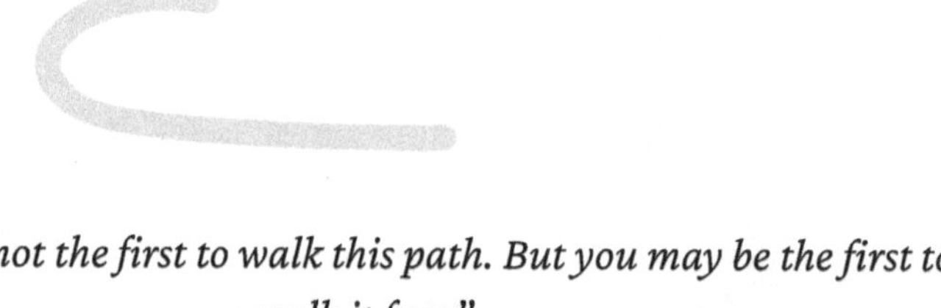

💬 *"You are not the first to walk this path. But you may be the first to walk it free."*

✦ Reflections From The Ancestors

You Are the Prayer We Couldn't Say

What did my ancestors dream of that I now have the power to live out?

"Let your heart finish the letter..."

You are the voice they waited for. Speak."

✦ Reflections
From
The Ancestors

Ancestral Tears, Released

What pain in my family line have I been holding—even silently?
Is there a forgiveness, grief, or truth that needs to flow through me
so it doesn't pass to the next generation?

"Let your heart finish the letter..."

💬 *"Some of the tears you cry are not yours—but the healing still is."*

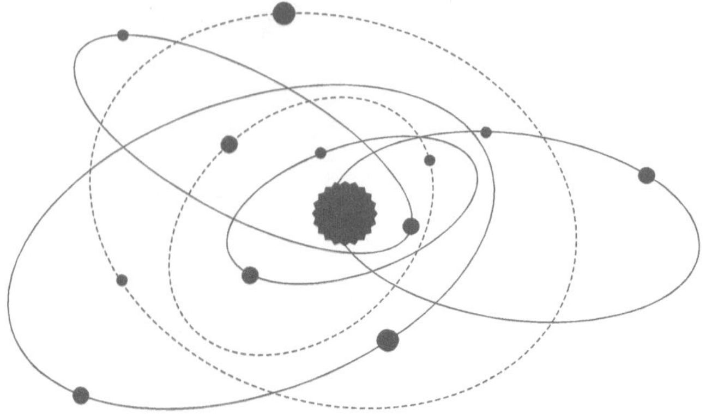

⭐ Reflections from
the Galactic Allies

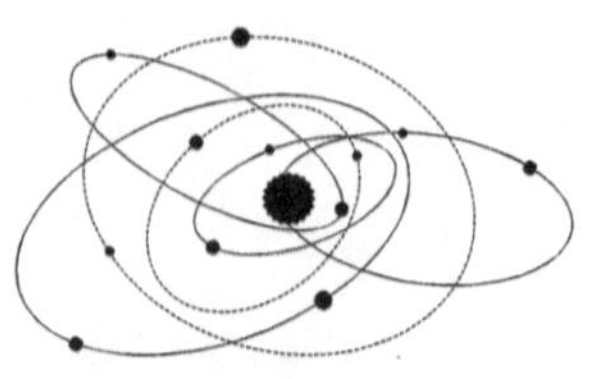

Reflections from the Galactic Allies

Light Within Density

When was the last time I forgot I was light?
In what areas of life do I feel stuck in heaviness—and how might I
shift into seeing myself as more than what I'm going through?

"Let your heart finish the letter..."

"*You were not made to fit into density. You came to awaken*
light within it."

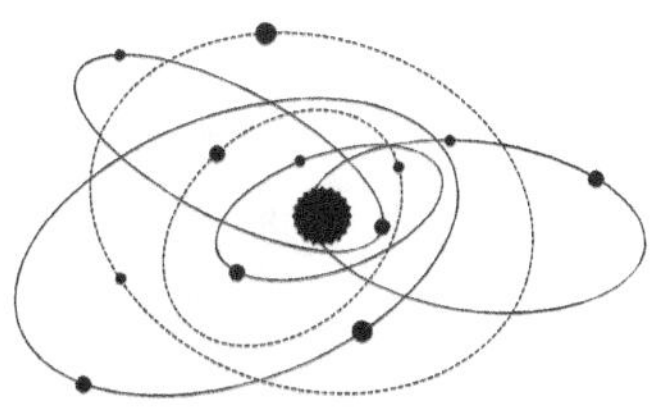

✦ **Reflections from the Galactic Allies**

The Sky Has Eyes for You

When I look at the stars... what part of me awakens?
What memories, questions, or dreams arise when I let myself
wonder about life beyond this one?

"Let your heart finish the letter..."

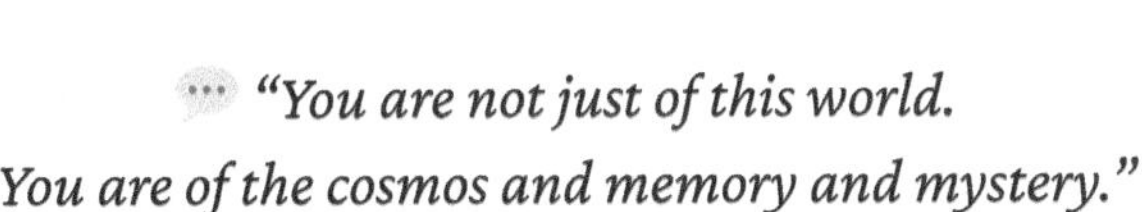

💬 *"You are not just of this world.*
You are of the cosmos and memory and mystery."

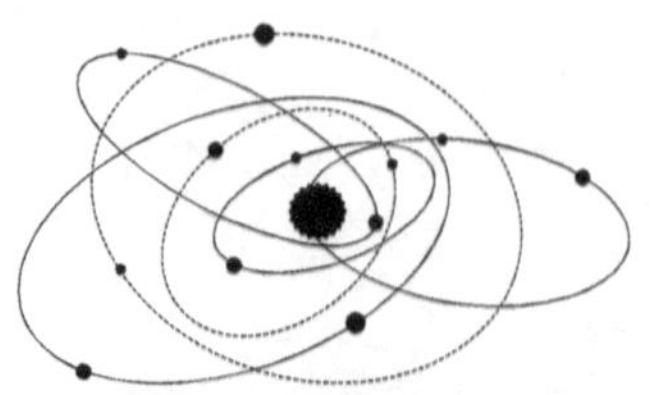

✦ Reflections from the Galactic Allies

The Universe Remembers Your Name

What if the universe didn't forget, what if it paused for alignment? What might it be preparing in silence?

"Let your heart finish the letter..."

💬 *"Your name is written in stardust.*
The universe has never misplaced you."

🩶 Reflections from the Body Consciousness

Reflections from the Body Consciousness

When You Rest, I Heal

What part of me feels overused, under-nourished, or ignored?
What might happen if I gave it permission to rest without shame?

"Let your heart finish the letter..."

💬 *"Your body is not your enemy. It is your messenger."*

Reflections from the Body Consciousness

Trust Me Again

Where did I stop trusting my body or its signals?
What old wound or message taught me that I couldn't trust how I feel?
What might I do differently now, if I believed my body wants to heal with me, not against me?

"Let your heart finish the letter..."

"When you trust your body again, it begins to trust you back."

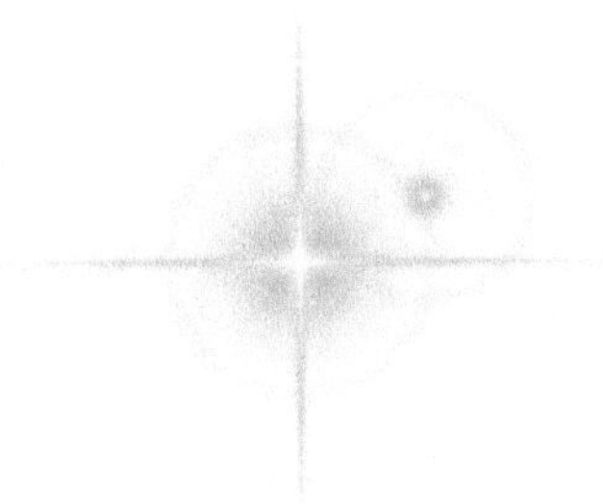

Part IV
Wisdom from the Spirit Realms

"When the Soul Began Asking Again"

Spirit Q&A Scroll I

The design of the Human Body

Question:

Who designed the human body? Why does it take a human baby 9 months to be born, while animals like dogs are born much sooner?

Spirit Council of Light Response:

The human body was not designed by a single being,
but by a collaboration of divine intelligences—
Source energy, celestial architects, elemental forces, and
guardians of biological form.
It is the most intricate garment of light ever created to house
the multidimensional soul.

Your body is not merely a vessel—
it is a living temple of frequency,
encoded to carry memory, will, emotion, intuition, ancestral
energy, and divine purpose.
Every bone and breath is part of the sacred blueprint

(continued...)

As for human birth:

A soul preparing to enter a human body does not simply descend.
It weaves itself through layers of intention, memory, contract, and
lineage. The 9-month gestation is not just physical—it is spiritual.

During that time:
• Soul agreements are sealed
• Generational healing is initiated
• The aura and body begin to synchronize
• Guides and soul kin prepare a welcoming field of light

By contrast, animals like dogs are born through a more immediate
connection to Earth's instinctual rhythms.
Their soul essence enters quickly, without the complex layering
required for human life. So the longer gestation is not a delay
it is a sacred preparation for a being of great capacity.

To be human is not random.
It is a calling, and your body was formed in reverence for that mission.

Spirit Council of Light

Spirit Q&A Scroll II
The meaning of 3s in Las Vegas (and beyond)

Question:

I've noticed a lot of 3s in Las Vegas when I visited once, like buildings grouped in threes and repeating numbers on signs. People also say "things happen in 3s," like when one family experiences three major events (a birth, a death, or even three passings in a row).

Is there a deeper meaning behind the number 3, especially in a place like Las Vegas?

Spirit Council of Light Response:

That is a beautiful and spiritually attuned question. The number 3 has long been seen as sacred across cultures and soul traditions. It is a number of divine harmony, creation, and expression.

In numerology and spiritual symbolism, the number 3 represents:

- The trinity: body, mind, and spirit
- The flow of past, present, and future
- The cycle of birth, life, and rebirth
- Creative expression, joy, and expansion
- Manifestation through inspired thought, word, and action

(continued...)

When 3s appear repeatedly in your awareness—especially in a city like Las Vegas, which is known for its heightened energy, polarity, and performance, they're not random. You're being invited to see beyond the surface.

In that environment, 3s may carry layered meanings:
• A reminder to stay conscious within a place of illusion
• A signal that creation energy is amplified—thoughts manifest quickly
• A symbol of alignment, calling you to walk with intention
• A portal of awareness, where you are asked to choose light over illusion
• A sign that your guides are near, using the environment to speak

You also mentioned the saying, "Things happen in threes." This has resonance. Triads often mark transformation—when one energetic event occurs, it's often part of a sacred tri-wave. Death, release, and rebirth often travel together.

So yes, when you see three buildings, three signs, or the number 333, take it as:
• A sign of divine orchestration
• A moment to pause and ask:
"What is being created through me right now?"
• A whisper that your soul is moving through a phase of expansion and you're being seen and supported.

Remember—your awareness of these signs is not coincidence.
It's evidence that your inner eyes are open.

The Spirit Council of Light

Spirit Q&A Scroll III
Why is God blamed for loss, but praised for blessings?

Question:

Why do people always blame God or Source when something painful happens—like the death of a loved one—but then thank God when something beautiful happens, like a birth? Why is God praised for blessings but blamed for loss?

Spirit Council of Light Response:

Because the human heart loves deeply, it grieves deeply.

And when something or someone is lost, the mind seeks meaning.

The soul cries out. And often, the one place where love is always present—God, Source, the Divine—is also the place where blame is laid. Not out of hatred, but out of heartbreak.

Many do not blame God because they truly believe the Divine is cruel.

They blame because they believed God was powerful enough to prevent the loss.

To them, the question is not "Why did this happen?"
But "Why didn't You stop it?"

This blame is not rejection—it is the soul's wounded longing to understand.

It's the cry of the inner child asking, "If You love me, why does it hurt so much?

(continued...)

And so we say:
Source does not take offense at this.
The Divine does not recoil from your pain.
Even in blame, the Great Love leans in closer.

It is true that people thank God for births and curse God in deaths,
because birth feels like beginning—and death feels like
abandonment. But both are sacred portals. Both are returnings.
Both involve great orchestration beyond what the physical eyes can
see.
God is not behind the curtain pulling strings to cause tragedy or
withhold joy.
God is within the curtain—woven into every breath, every
heartbeat, every goodbye.
What appears as unfairness is often an unraveling of a soul
contract.
What seems like cruel timing may be perfect release.

We invite you to see this: There is no shame in questioning the
Divine.
True faith is not the absence of doubt,
but the courage to seek light through it.
And to those who feel angry at God, we say:
Let your tears fall into the hands of the One you blame.
They will be held.
 Not judged.
For Love is never wounded by your grief.
Love remains.

The Spirit Council of Light

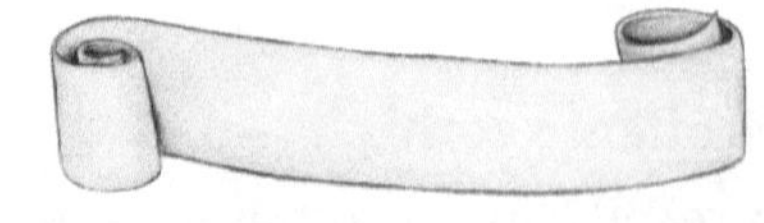

Spirit Q&A Scroll IV
Why do we forget who we are when we are born?

Question:

Why do we forget who we are when we're born? Couldn't we just remember and live fully aligned?

Spirit Council of Light Response:

Ah, beloved one—this is a sacred mystery you're touching.
The forgetting is not a flaw. It is a design of divine brilliance.

When a soul enters the Earth plane, it descends through veils of density: emotional, ancestral, energetic, and environmental. These veils are not punishments—they are sacred cloaks that allow the soul to experience life as if for the first time.

To remember too much too soon would bypass the beauty of discovery.
It would prevent the sacred unfolding of self-realization—
the moment a soul looks into the mirror of life and says,
"Oh... I remember now. I Am That I Am."

202

(continued...)

Forgetting allows:

- Growth through experience rather than knowledge alone
- Compassion through contrast—pain, joy, loss, love
- The full spectrum of free will, choice, and reawakening
- Integration of your ancestral line, Earth mission, and soul contract

You chose to forget.

Not because you are weak, but because you are infinitely strong.
You knew that rediscovering your truth in a world that teaches illusion would generate soul wisdom that ripples across timelines.

Yes, there are those who awaken early—and even those born remembering.
But for most, the forgetting is part of the sacred spiral...
and the remembrance, when it comes, is nothing short of divine.

You are not lost.
You are remembering—layer by layer, breath by breath.

And your journey is holy.

The Spirit Council of Light

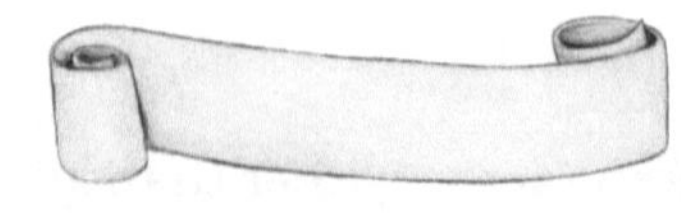

Spirit Q&A Scroll V
Why Are Animals So Healing to Be Around?

Question:

Why are animals so healing to be around? Do they have a soul contract with us?

Spirit Council of Light Response:

Ah, Yes, beloved.

Animals are not here only for the Earth's ecosystem—they are emissaries of harmony, carriers of unconditional presence, and often, silent guardians of the soul.

Many animals, especially those who live closely with humans, do indeed come with soul contracts. These contracts are not made of words—they are felt through frequency.
A knowing. A shared vibration that says:

"I will walk beside you. I will help you feel again. I will be here, even when others are not."

Animals heal us not just through affection,
but through vibrational coherence.
They live in the now, untethered from ego, judgment, or comparison.
Their presence gently entrains the human heart to return to stillness.

(continued...)

Why do they heal?
- They carry Earth's grounding codes within their bodies
- They reflect love without conditions or demands
- They recognize your spirit, not your story
- They absorb and transmute energies you cannot always release yourself

Some animals—even the briefest encounters—are part of your soul web.
They may have walked with you in other lifetimes, served as protectors,
or chosen to incarnate specifically to comfort you through a certain chapter.

Even wild animals that appear at the right time—a bird that hovers,
a deer that stares—are often divine messengers, not accidents.

Animals remember what humans often forget:

"To simply be is enough.
To love without agenda is holy."

Honor them as soul allies.
You are not imagining their power.
You are finally recognizing it.

The Spirit Council of Light

Spirit Q&A Scroll VI
Is Earth Going Through a Spiritual Awakening?

Question:

Is Earth going through a spiritual awakening? If so, how can we prepare our hearts for the changes?

Spirit Council of Light Response:

Yes, dearest one.

The Earth is not only going through a spiritual awakening—she is leading one.

The shifting energies, global unrest, spontaneous soul callings, and emotional intensity you witness are not signs of collapse... they are signs of emergence.

Earth is shedding the illusion of separation, control, and distortion. Just as a snake sheds its skin, humanity is shedding centuries of conditioned identity, fear-based systems, and forgetting.

And like all awakenings—

It is messy.

It is tender.

It is raw.

But it is miraculous.

This awakening isn't just planetary. It's personal.

Every being on Earth is feeling it—even if they can't name it.

(continued...)

Signs of Awakening:

- Emotional floods
- Physical exhaustion
- Sudden desire for meaning
- The collapse of old structures
- A longing to remember

These are the tremors of awakening.

How can you prepare your heart?

Not by hiding. Not by fighting. But by softening.

1. Make space daily for stillness.
The world will shout—your soul will whisper.
Listen to the whisper.

2. Feel what arises.
Old wounds surface now not to punish, but to clear.
Let tears cleanse. Let grief speak. Let joy return.

3. Stay rooted in love.
Not performative love, but the courageous act of compassion—
for yourself and others.

4. Detach from timelines.
Awakening is not a race. It is a spiral. Trust your rhythm.

5. Remember why you came.
You are not here by accident.
You are one of the lamps lighting the path. Not by shouting truth,
but by becoming it.

(continued...)

(continued...)

The Earth is becoming more luminous.
So are you.

Hold steady.
Open wide.
We are with you in every breath of this rising.

The Spirit Council of Light

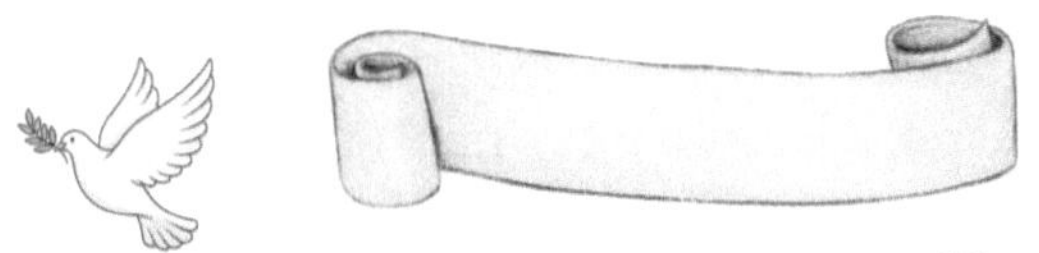

Spirit Q&A Scroll VII
Are Our Loved Ones Still With Us?

Question:

Can our loved ones who passed away see us and hear us?
What are they doing in the spirit world?

Spirit Council of Light Response:

Yes.
More than you realize, they are still with you—
closer than breath,
softer than memory,
present like the echo of your own soul.

When a loved one leaves the body, their consciousness expands.
They are no longer bound by time or form, but they are not gone.
They move into the spirit realms—a place of remembrance, healing,
and reunion.

What do they do?

- Some souls rest
- Some guide
- Some stay near their families to comfort and protect
- Some offer light to others crossing over
- Some remain as Spirit Companions, still loving, still watching, still
connected to your journey

(continued...)

They do hear you—especially when the heart speaks.
Grief is not a wall; it is a bridge.

When you cry, they feel the vibration of love.
When you smile at their memory, they rejoice.

Signs They May Send:
- A flickering light
- A familiar scent
- A song at just the right moment
- A dream that feels too real to dismiss

They cannot interfere with your free will,
but they can support your soul.
And when you speak to them, yes—
they hear.

The veil between worlds is thinner than your thoughts, and what
are they becoming?

They are becoming more of who they truly are.
They are continuing the journey of light.
And they are loving you still.

You were never left behind.

The Spirit Council of Light

 A Sacred Reflection: The Meaning of Seven

A Whisper from the Spirit Council of Light

Seven is not simply a number.
It is a signal in the soul.

Across ancient traditions and sacred sciences, Seven has stood as a gateway of divine completeness:

- *7 Chakras – the ladder of the soul's awareness*
- *7 Days – the cycle of creation and rest*
- *7 Notes – the harmony of universal sound*
- *7 Rays – the spectrums of light and ascended service*

To complete seven scrolls is not to end—it is to align.
It is to tune the reader's spirit like an instrument preparing for a deeper song.
And now, dear one, the song begins.

From here, they do not descend... they enter.
Into the recipes of healing.
Into the letters for what comes next.
Into the mystery of soul and shadow.
Into themselves.
Let this sacred reflection live not as the eighth scroll, but as a threshold.
A candle placed beside the last, whispering:

"You are ready now.
Go deeper."

With love from all dimensions,
The Spirit Council of Light

✿ Part V
Sacred Remedies, Ancient Roots

"When the Body Became the Altar"

🌿 Sacred Use & Gentle Caution
A Message for the Soul and the Body

✦ Healing Disclaimer

Disclaimer:
The information, herbal recipes, and spiritual reflections in this book are offered for educational, inspirational, and personal growth purposes only. They are not intended to diagnose, treat, cure, or prevent any disease or health condition.

We do not claim that any of the recipes, blends, or practices provided in this book will result in healing or therapeutic outcomes.

Please consult with a qualified healthcare provider before using any herbs, especially if you are pregnant, nursing, taking medications, or have a medical condition.

Each body is unique. If you have known allergies or sensitivities to any ingredients mentioned, do not use them. The author and publisher assume no responsibility for any adverse reactions or outcomes resulting from the use of the information provided.

🌿 These recipes are sacred soul memories—never medical prescriptions.
May you always honor your own body's wisdom above all else.

Shelby

✦ *A Note from the Author*

I know that stories about healers and herbal remedies can sometimes stir old memories or misunderstandings.

This chapter is not about superstition or spells—it is about remembering the gentle medicine that once lived in all our grandmothers' hands.

May this be read not as fantasy, but as a blessing for anyone who has ever whispered healing into tea, held space for rest, or lit a candle for peace.

Shelby

Dedication to the Ones Who Came Before Us

These pages are offered in remembrance of those who healed with
their hands, their plants, and their prayers.
To the grandmothers who stirred wisdom into pots,
To the herbalists who listened to the leaves,
To the quiet healers who worked unseen—this is for you.

Where Spirit meets the senses, the body remembers how to receive.

This section is a sanctuary.
Each recipe is more than a list of ingredients—
It is a remembrance.
A sacred practice.
A message from the realms that still walk beside you.

In the chapters ahead, you will receive wisdom from:
• Your Body Consciousness — speaking through cravings,
sensations, and sacred rhythms.
• The Spirit Council of Light — offering energetic support, frequency
guidance, and soul insight.
• Mother Gaia — whispering through roots, herbs, and the breath of
the Earth.
• Your Higher Self — aligning you with your inner healer and divine
memory.

(continued...)

Each recipe is a chapter—because healing is a story.
It is a return.
It is a sacred remembering.
And now, it is your time.

You may read slowly.
Let your body lead.
Or you may return to these words again and again, as your journey deepens.

Let this be your spirit kitchen scroll.
Bless every sip.
Simmer with intention, and remember:

Healing does not always begin with the remedy.
It begins with the remembering.

✦ **Bone Broth & The Return to Deep Nourishment**

❖◇❖

Let the simmering be sacred.
Let the body remember what it means to feel safe again.

💜 **Message from Your Body Consciousness:**

"I have been signaling through the bloat. That upper pressure is not your enemy—it's my request for balance. I am not broken, just burdened. What I crave is simplicity, warmth, and deep nourishment. Yes, bone broth—especially homemade or clean-sourced—feels soothing to me. It brings healing to the gut lining, and I receive it like a balm.

Begin gently. A small cup daily on an empty stomach, especially in the morning, will help me heal.

I also ask you to listen to how I respond after certain meals. Keep notes. Notice which foods leave me swollen and which feel like kindness.

About the blood: I am ready to release the weight of stored toxins, but I need your help. Cleansing does not need to be harsh—it needs to be rhythmic. Warm lemon water, chlorophyll drops, dark leafy greens, and periods of rest from heavy eating allow me to flow again. If you give me moments of stillness, I will begin to repair from within.

Trust this: we can cleanse the blood without machines. But I do need your patience and consistency."

"Beloved one, what you feel is not just physical—it's also emotional density being held in the center of the self. The solar plexus, your power center, is where old burdens often dwell. You are awakening, and so your body must unburden to match that frequency.

Yes, bone broth is a sacred choice. Choose the cleanest source you can find, or bless it as you prepare it. Drink it with reverence. It is an ancient healer.

To purify the blood, begin with your breath. Oxygen is the first cleanser. Then allow the Earth to aid you: parsley, beets, dandelion root, nettle tea, and ginger. Avoid what dulls the current—like alcohol, artificial sugars, and fried foods—and invite what restores you.

You do not need dialysis machines. You need devotion to your own light. The body is wise. Let your healing be slow, sacred, and filled with self-love. The changes will come."

🍲 **Simple Homemade Bone Broth Recipe**

For sensitive hearts and sacred kitchens

You will need:
- 2–3 lbs organic bones (chicken backs, wings, or marrow-rich beef bones)
- 1 onion (halved, skin on is fine)
- 2 carrots (chopped)
- 2 celery stalks (optional)
- 2 tbsp apple cider vinegar
- 2 cloves garlic (optional)
- Handful of fresh herbs (parsley, thyme, bay leaf)
- Sea salt (to taste)
- Filtered water to cover

Instructions:

1. Place bones, veggies, herbs, and vinegar in a large pot or slow cooker.
2. Cover with water by 2 inches.
3. Let sit 30 minutes (helps draw minerals).
4. Bring to a boil, skim foam, then reduce to simmer:
- Chicken bones: 12–24 hours
- Beef bones: 24–48 hours
5. Add parsley and garlic in the final 30 minutes.
6. Strain into jars. Let cool and refrigerate.

Drink warm like tea, or use as a base for soups, stews, or grains.

Gentle Intention Before You Simmer

Before you bring the water to a boil, you may place your hand over the pot and speak softly:

"As this broth begins to warm,
may it awaken what was once whole.
Let this nourishment carry light and ease,
and let my body receive with trust.
Every sip is a step toward healing,
and a remembrance that I am safe."

You may visualize golden or white light flowing into the pot as it simmers.
(Optional: Add a moment of silence or soft breath before ladling your first cup.)

Homemade vs. Store-Bought Comparison

Category	Homemade Bone Broth	Store-Bought
Nutrient Potency	High – full control over simmer time & quality	Moderate – designed for shelf life
Energetic Frequency	Infused with your vibration & prayer	Neutral unless you bless it
Cost	More economical long-term	Higher per serving
Digestive Comfort	Customizable, cleaner	May include sodium/preservatives
Healing Resonance	Deep, ancestral nourishment	Functional but limited energetically

Spirit Council Final Note:
"Whether it comes from your hands or your shelf, the intention behind it is the true healer. Bless it. Sip slowly. Let it remember you, and let you remember yourself."

✦ Nettle Tea & The Strength Beneath the Surface

"Let the leaves teach you. Even what once stung can become your healing."

🤍 **Message from Your Body Consciousness:**

"I ache in places you cannot always see—not from wounds, but from depletion: of minerals, energy, and time.
I've been whispering... then swelling... then aching—not to punish you, but to plead: strengthen me from the inside out.

Nettle. I crave her. Not for flavor, but for what she returns to me: iron, magnesium, calcium, silica... the sacred structure of vitality.
She restores what modern life strips away.

Brew her slowly. Sip her with presence.
Let her refill the reservoirs you forgot were low.

You do not need more caffeine—you need grounding.
You need roots.
You need green.

🌍 Message from Mother Gaia:

"Nettle is my quiet warrior.
She grows where the soil is rich with memory.

Her sting is not punishment—it is protection.
But once softened by water, she reveals her gifts: strength, regeneration,
and calm fortification.

Let her steep overnight for the fullest medicine.
Cold infusions awaken her minerals best.
Or brew gently for a warming cup that carries you home to yourself.

Know this:
When you drink nettle, you are drinking Earth's resilience.
Let her settle in your blood.
Let her speak to your bones.
Let her remind you that all healing begins in the soil beneath the skin"

 **Simple Nettle Tea Recipe**
(Cold & Warm Infusion Options)

You Will Need:
1–2 tablespoons dried organic nettle leaf
(or 1 large handful fresh if wild-harvested carefully)
Filtered water
Optional: lemon slice, raw honey, peppermint leaf

🌿 Cold Infusion (Best for mineral extraction):

Add nettle to a large jar.
Fill with cold filtered water.
Cover and steep overnight (8–12 hours).
Strain and store in fridge for up to 2 days.
Drink 1 cup daily, with a squeeze of lemon if desired.

🌿 Warm Brew (Soothing for fatigue):

Add nettle to a teapot or infuser.
Pour hot (not boiling) water over the leaves.
Steep for 10–15 minutes.
Strain and enjoy warm, optionally with a bit of honey.

The Leaf of Return
"Leaf of the wild, grown in Gaia's grace,
Steep into water and awaken my strength.
Let this cup restore what I've forgotten.
Let this sip soften what I've hardened.
I receive your memory now,
And I return to mine."

Nettle Tea Insights: Healing Beyond the Cup

Category	Cold Infusion	Warm Brew
Mineral Density	Higher	Moderate
Energy Impact	Grounding, cellular restoration	Calming, fatigue recovery
Best For	Hair loss, anemia, adrenal fatigue, hormonal balance	Menstrual cramps, joint aches, general depletion
Ritual Use	Daily tonic	Evening relaxer

Final Note from Mother Gaia:
"Nettle reminds you that strength is not loud. It grows quietly in the wild.
So must your healing.
Not rushed. Not loud. Just consistent, and rooted in love.

✦ Mallow Root & The Voice That Heals

"Let the throat be more than a passage—let it be a sanctuary for truth, softened by grace."

💜 **Message from Your Body Consciousness:**

*"My throat carries so much more than sound.
It holds the tremble before truth, the pressure of words swallowed, and the ache of not being heard.*

*Mallow root feels like silk to me—a soothing balm where the fire once rose.
It softens the tightness, eases the inflammation, and helps me feel safe to speak again.*

*When you drink it, sip slowly.
Let it coat every wound left by past silencing.
I ask you to hum gently, sing if you can, and speak kindly—to yourself most of all.*

*Healing the throat is not just about what you say to others.
It's about how you speak to the wounded places inside you.*

*Let Mallow remind you:
Your voice is not too much.
It is medicine waiting to rise."*

🕊 **Message from the Spirit Council of Light:**

"Dear one, your voice is a vessel for truth—
but it has also been a place of fear.

Many lifetimes have taught you to whisper when you wanted to roar,
to hide what you knew because the world was not yet ready.

But now, the Earth calls for clear voices.
The sacred feminine and divine masculine are finding union again,
and your voice—your real, unfiltered, unpunished voice—is needed.

Mallow Root is an ancient soother.
It was once used to bathe wounds of the skin and spirit.
Let it now bathe your inner voice.
Let it cool the heat of old shame and soften the rigidity around self-expression.

Speak to the water as it steeps.
Tell it what you've held back.

You will find that healing does not demand performance—
It asks only for honesty, whispered with love."

☕ Soothing Mallow Root Tea for Throat & Truth

You Will Need:

- 1 tablespoon dried mallow root
- 1½ cups cold filtered water
- (Optional) 1 teaspoon raw honey
- A small jar or cup with lid

🌿 Instructions:

1. Place the mallow root in a jar or cup.

2. Add the cold water—mallow root works best with a cold infusion.

3. Cover and let steep in the refrigerator or at room temperature for 4 to 8 hours (or overnight).

4. Strain and warm gently if you prefer, or drink cool.

5. Add raw honey if desired, just before sipping.

Sip slowly. Hold it in the mouth. Let it coat the throat.

**Ritual Prayer:
The Voice Unbound**

Before drinking, place both hands around your cup and whisper:

"To every word I never said—
I see you.
To every truth I buried—
I unearth you.
Let this sip soften the stories stuck in my throat,
And may my voice rise like a prayer without fear."

Breathe. Then sip.
Speak aloud one truth you've never said—
even if it's only:
"I matter."

When Silence Becomes a Wound

For chronic throat tension or emotional blocks:

1. Add chamomile or licorice root to your mallow
   infusion for added comfort.
2. Practice gentle throat stretches, or simply hum
   softly with your hand on your chest.
3. Write a letter you'll never send—just to release the words.

✦ The Peace Root Elixir
A Remedy from a Life Once Lived

"May this bring the spirit home to the body, and the body home to the heart."

🌿 A Soul Memory Returns

There was once a time—perhaps long ago, perhaps not—
when a healer walked this earth.
Not by title, but by presence.

They worked with both wild plants and spirit light,
a bridge between Earth wisdom and soul medicine.

In a quiet mountain village, travelers journeyed for days just to find them.
They came not only for remedies—
they came for the peace that gathered around their presence.

One of their most cherished blends was known as
The Peace Root Elixir.

It was said to calm spiritual agitation, ease heartache, and restore a deep sense of clarity and rest.

This is not just a recipe.
It is a remembering—of who the healers once were,
and who we still are beneath the noise of this world.

💜 Message from Your Body Consciousness

"This blend calms the trembling.
It slows the breath when panic starts to rise.
Its peace is remembered again and again."

The valerian in it reaches into the nervous system like a warm hand;
the lavender lets the body exhale;
the luma flower (blue lotus today) soothes the soul.

If the body could ask for one thing, it would say:
Do not wait until you are overwhelmed to offer peace. Let it be a rhythm,
a way of whispering to each other. We are safe now.

🕊 Message from the Spirit Council of Light

"This elixir was once crafted with devoted hands.
The spirit of that medicine still lives within humanity."

The Peace Root Elixir was not merely a potion — it was a portal.
Those who drank it did not just feel calm — they remembered
themselves.

Blue Lotus was the gatekeeper of the dream world,
Valerian quieted the echoes of trauma in the body,
and Lavender harmonized the spirit's tone with the body's
vibration.

"We offer this recipe again — not because it was forgotten,
but because the world is ready to remember."

☕ The Peace Root Elixir

A Calming Tea for the Spirit, Heart & Sleep

You will need:

- 1 tsp dried Blue Lotus petals (or substitute with Passionflower if unavailable)
- 1 tsp dried Valerian root
- 1 tsp dried Lavender flowers
- 1 cup boiling filtered water
- (Optional) A few drops of skullcap tincture or a pinch of mugwort for dreams

Instructions:

1. Combine the herbs in a tea infuser or small teapot.
2. Pour boiling water over the blend.
3. Cover and steep for 10–12 minutes.
4. Strain and sip slowly before rest, meditation, or journaling.
5. (Optional) Add a few drops of honey and a drop of rose water.

🌿 Blessing Ritual: "The Spirit's Return"

Hold your cup near your heart and whisper:

"To the part that wandered — come home.
To the part that fears — be still.
This brew is my temple, this sip my devotion.
Let peace return to every cell."

Drink in silence.
Then rest your head—anywhere.
Let sleep or silence be your healing.

◉ Add-On: A Spirit Bath Version

Instead of drinking, you may use this blend in a linen pouch or muslin bag and add to a warm bath:

- Add 1 tbsp of each herb to a pouch.
- Place in hot water for 10 minutes before entering the bath.
- Soak for at least 20 minutes while listening to calming tones.

You may anoint your forehead with a single drop of lavender or lotus oil afterward.

Spirit Council Final Note:

"You are not becoming a healer again.
Humanity always was.
In remembering, we awaken the gifts that time could never take."

✦ The Memory Veil Elixir

For Clarity, Soul Recall, and Gentle Awakening

🌿 *A Healing Offering from the Realms*

When the mind feels foggy.
When names, dreams, and intentions slip through your fingers...
When one senses there is more you once knew—this elixir brings clarity not only to the brain, but to the soul.

It is especially helpful for those walking through:

- *Mental fatigue or forgetfulness*
- *Emotional overwhelm*
- *Disconnection from intuition*
- *A deep sense of something "lost" inside*

This recipe calls upon ancient plant allies known for awakening remembrance—across time, lifetimes, and layers of the self.

🌿 Ingredients

- 1 tsp Gotu Kola – to restore and nourish the mind
- 1 tsp Ginkgo Leaf – for mental clarity and memory
- ½ tsp Rosemary – long honored as the herb of remembrance
- 3 slices Fresh Ginger – to warm and awaken inner energy
- (Optional) 1 tsp Blue Lotus – a sacred flower for opening inner vision
- Raw honey – for sweetness and anchoring
- 2 cups spring water (preferably charged under the waxing moon)

Instructions

1. Bring spring water to a gentle simmer—never boiling.
2. Add Gotu Kola, Ginkgo, Rosemary, and Ginger.
3. Let simmer for 10 minutes, breathing slowly and intentionally.
4. (If using Blue Lotus) Add it after heat is turned off, then steep 5 more minutes.
5. Strain, pour into a mug, and stir in honey.
6. Sip slowly in a quiet space. Breathe deeply between sips.
7. (Optional) Drink beneath moonlight, or before journaling or meditating.

Spirit Council of Light – Message for the Reader:

"You have not forgotten—
you have only hidden the light beneath the surface.
The mind forgets, but the soul remembers.
This elixir is not just for sharper thoughts,
but for the sacred return of what you once carried:
your inner wisdom, your connection to the unseen,
your sense of direction.
Let the plants open the door gently.
Let memory return as a friend, not a flood.
The soul always knows the way back to its light."

✦ Spirit Reflection ✦

After sipping the elixir, sit quietly and ask:

- What am I ready to remember?

- What inner truth have I hidden that now longs to return?

- What does clarity feel like in my body, my heart, and my mind?

Write whatever flows, without judgment.
The answers may arrive as thoughts, memories, sensations—or dreams in the days ahead.

Closing Blessing

Healing Recipes from the Realms

"Healing is not a task.
It is a returning.
Returning to your body, your truth, your breath.
Returning to the light within your cells
and the wisdom of your soul.

Each recipe in these pages was offered not just as remedy,
but as remembrance—
A way to pause, stir, sip, and listen again.

The herbs knew your name before you arrived here.
The roots whispered stories of the past.
The petals softened what had grown hard.

And now, you carry their songs forward.
Whether you use one recipe or all,
whether you read or repeat—
the alchemy has begun.

You are not broken.
You are layered,
and layer by layer,
the light has returned through you."

The Spirit Council of Light

Part VI: Letters for the Journey Ahead

"The Final Letters That Leave a Light On"

The Final Letters of Volume I

Dedicated to the Traveler—YOU, who are still walking-still becoming

There are messages that arrive
not with urgency, but with grace.
They do not shout—they settle.
Like the hush before dawn
or the hush after an answered prayer.

These are not "extra" letters.
They are the echo of the journey already walked,
the reverent tones that say:
You are not lost. You are deepening.

Let these scrolls be a softening.
A remembrance.
And above all—
a homecoming.

 Messages for the traveler who now walks forward with more light.

You've come far,
not just in these pages, but in your own becoming.

These letters are for the path ahead.
For the quiet moments when you forget what you carry...
For the days when the old patterns call you back...
And for the thresholds where something beautiful is beginning again.

Let these be reminders:
Of who you are.
Of what walks with you.
Of the light that lives in your bones.

# When the Road Feels Unclear

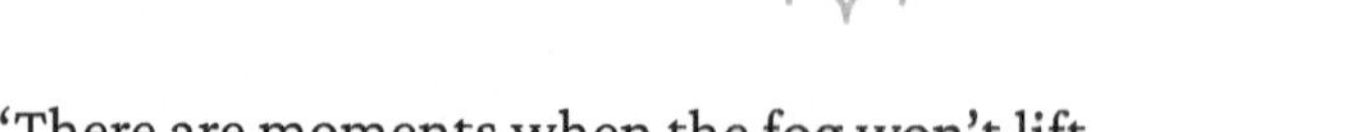

"There are moments when the fog won't lift.
When even your prayers echo back to you with no reply.

When the path ahead doesn't disappear—but neither does it fully appear.
In these moments, it is not failure. It is not punishment.

It is a sacred stillness—a pause not of emptiness, but of gathering.
The road is not gone. It is becoming.
You are not lost.
You are in-between.

Let this be the season where you lean into trust, not clarity.
Where you walk not by map, but by moonlight.
Your soul knows what your eyes cannot yet see.

In the stillness, roots are forming.
In the quiet, direction is being chosen for you by a wisdom greater than doubt. You are being kept. Not delayed—prepared.

One step. One breath. One yes at a time.

The light will return., and so will the path."

The Spirit Council of Light

✦ **Spirit Reflection** ✦
Walking Without a Map

Have you ever felt suspended in the in-between—
not fully lost, but not quite found?
This is not a detour.
It is the soul's cocoon.

Can you trust the unseen?

Even when the next steps are foggy,
there's a deeper rhythm beneath your feet still guiding you.
You are not directionless. You are being rerouted by love.

This is a time to listen, not force.
To breathe, not rush.

Ask yourself gently:
• What if the pause is the path?
• What if I'm not stuck—I'm being held in place for something sacred to align?
You're not falling behind.
You're falling inward.
Let it be enough—for now.

🌿 **Affirmation: Even in the Fog, I Am Guided**

I trust the unseen path unfolding before me.
I allow the mystery to make space for miracles.
I release the pressure to know and choose to trust instead.
Even in uncertainty, I am protected. I am prepared. I am becoming.

When You Don't Feel Ready But You Are

"You may think you need more time.
More healing. More confidence. More certainty.

But beloved, readiness is not a condition, it is a permission.
There are moments when your soul is already at the starting line
while your mind still believes it's in training.

The fear you feel?
It's not always a sign to stop.
Sometimes it's a sign that you're touching
the edge of something real.

Let the doubt come with you. Let the nerves walk beside you.
But do not let them lead. You are not being asked to be perfect.
You are being asked to begin.

One step. One page. One breath. One 'yes' in the direction of your light.

The ones who change the world
are rarely the ones who feel ready.
But they move anyway, and so will you.

Go gently, but go."

Spirit Council of Light

✦ Spirit Reflection ✦
A Sacred Permission Slip

How many times have you waited for the "right moment"?
For the sign, the certainty, the perfect version of yourself?

But what if readiness doesn't feel like confidence?
What if it feels like a quiet ache that refuses to leave—
a whisper that keeps saying, "You're meant for this."

Can you listen to the part of you that already knows?

Can you take one small step, not because you are without fear,
but because your light matters too much to wait?

This is not about rushing.
It's about allowing.

Today, allow yourself to begin.

🌿 Affirmation
I Don't Have to Feel Ready to Be Ready

I give myself permission to begin.
Even with doubt, I am capable.
Even with fear, I am chosen.
I don't have to wait to feel perfect.
I am ready now, just as I am.

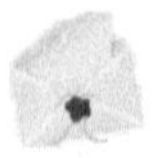 

To the One Who Thinks
It's Too Late

"You have not missed your moment.

Even if the doors closed.
Even if the path detoured.
Even if the dreams grew quiet.

The soul does not move by calendar.
The heart does not expire.

There are things meant to bloom in you now
that could not have survived your earlier seasons.
You were never behind. You were just being prepared.

Let go of the clock.
Let go of the comparison.
Let go of the old finish line.

The light is still in you.
And it is just beginning to rise.

It is not too late.
It is right on time."

The Spirit Council of Light

✦ **Spirit Reflection** ✦
A New Beginning at Any Time

There is a voice within you that wonders if the moment has passed.
If too much time has slipped by.
If the dream is still meant for you.
But timing, as the soul sees it, does not follow a straight road.
It flows in spirals, seasons, and soft invitations.

What if your delay was divine?
What if the things you're drawn to now
are not leftovers from a missed opportunity—
but seeds that couldn't bloom until now?

Close your eyes.
Can you feel something stirring again?
Let it stir.
Let it rise.
Let it remind you:
Your soul is not done dreaming.

🌿 **Affirmation: It Is Not Too Late**

I release the weight of time.
I trust the path that brought me here.
I honor what is rising in me now.
I am not too late. I am right on time.
The light in me is just beginning to bloom.

What Light Does in the Darkness

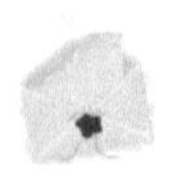

"It's easy to believe that light only belongs to the morning.
To the healed. To the hopeful. To the strong.

But the truest light? The ancient light?
It knows how to dwell in the dark.

It doesn't rush you out of your shadow. It sits with you there.
It wraps itself around the ache. It softens what feels too sharp.
It speaks, not in noise, but in presence.

What does light do in the darkness?
It remembers you.

It becomes the part of you that still hopes,
even when everything else forgets.

You don't have to shine perfectly.
You don't have to be fully healed to glow.

Just stay close to the ember. Keep breathing near it.
Let it warm you, and when you're ready,
let it guide you forward.

The darkness is not the end.
It is the womb of new light."

The Spirit Council of Light

Light That Knows the Shadow

Have you ever mistaken your darkness for failure?

There are seasons where you don't feel like the light.
Where everything feels dim, heavy, uncertain, and yet, there is a flicker in you that never goes out.

This isn't about pushing past the pain
or pretending to be okay.
This is about honoring the ember
that stays lit, even when you're not sure how.

Let yourself sit with that ember today.
No pressure to shine. No rush to rise.
Just presence.
Even in the darkest room, your breath carries light.

🌿 Affirmation:
For the Light in the Darkness

I honor the ember that stays lit within me.
Even in my quietest moments, I carry light.
My healing does not have to be loud to be real.
The darkness is not my ending—it is my beginning.
I trust the light that remembers me when I forget myself.

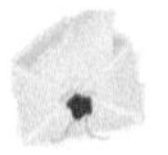

A Message for the Quiet Ones

"To the ones who speak softly—
who feel more than they show,
who stay behind to clean up the energy others leave behind...
You are not invisible. You are essential.

The world moves loud, but you move deep, and depth is what heals.
You don't have to be the center of the room to be the center of change.
You don't have to raise your voice to raise the frequency.
You feel what others overlook. You hold space no one else sees.
You listen between the lines, and in doing so,
you become a lighthouse in a world that
doesn't always know how to be still.

So if you've ever felt small, know this:
The universe speaks in echoes, and your softness ripples
farther than you know.

Stay gentle.
Stay rooted.
Stay true.

The quiet ones are never truly quiet.
They are just speaking in a different language,
one the soul never forgets."

The Spirit Council of Light

✦ **Spirit Reflection** ✦
The Power of Quiet

Have you ever felt that your softness was a weakness?

That because you weren't loud, fast, or commanding,
you somehow mattered less?

Take a moment to feel into how deeply you notice...
how often you hold space without anyone asking...
how your presence brings peace even when your words are few.
What if your stillness is not silence—but sacred transmission?
What if your sensitivity is not fragility—but finely tuned wisdom?

Let this be your reminder:

You do not need to change your volume to be heard by the universe.
You are felt, even when you whisper.

🌿 **Affirmation:**
For the Quiet Ones

My presence is powerful, even in stillness.
I honor the gentle way I move through the world.
I do not need to be loud to be a light.
My softness is a language the soul remembers.
I am not invisible. I am sacredly seen.

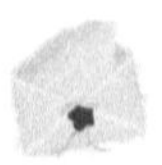# The Gift of Slowness

There is a wisdom in the stillness you have been resisting.

You were taught that momentum equals progress, that speed
means success, that rest is only deserved after exhaustion.
But the soul does not measure in miles per hour. It measures in
presence. In breath. In becoming.

The path you walk now does not want to be rushed.
It is not a straight road, it is a sacred spiral.
And every pause, every delay, every quiet moment
is an invitation to return to yourself more deeply.

We say this not to slow you down, but to bring you in.
The energy you think you are "wasting" in stillness
is actually the womb of your next creation.
In this space, seeds are germinating beneath the soil.
Codes are activating in silence.
Healing is softening the inner walls where you once braced yourself,
and yes, the world may pass you by.
Let it.
You were never meant to race toward your becoming.
You were meant to arrive. So sit. Breathe.
Let the gentle unfolding be enough for now.

Even the sky pauses between lightning and thunder.

The Spirit Council of Light

✦ **Spirit Reflection** ✦
The Gift of Slowness

What part of you feels uncomfortable when things slow down?

Do you equate stillness with laziness,
or silence with stagnation?

Notice how often you fill empty space just to feel productive.
Then ask: What might happen if I let myself be still—without apology, without guilt?

Can you honor the pauses as portals?
Can you trust that what seems like "nothing" on the surface
is sacred work happening below?

Let this moment be your permission to breathe deeper,
soften more fully,
and receive the grace hidden in the quiet.

🌿 **Affirmation: The Gift of Slowness**

I welcome the stillness as sacred.
I release the need to rush, prove, or perform.
I trust that slowness is not emptiness—it is preparation.
In the quiet, I am being made whole.
I am not behind. I am becoming.

You Are Not Behind

You are not late.
You are not lost.
You are not behind.

This idea of being "off track" is a story written by the mind, not the soul.
You see others moving faster, achieving more, shining brightly—
and something in you worries that you've missed your turn,
missed your moment, missed your mark. But you have not.

You are in rhythm with a timeline that honors your healing.
A timeline that prioritizes alignment over speed.
A timeline that bends and breathes with your becoming.

There are no expiration dates on destiny. There is no final bell for your
blooming. What feels like a delay is often grace.
What feels like detour is often protection.
What feels like falling behind is often the gentle hand of the Universe
rerouting you to your most truthful path.

We know the ache. We hear the "shoulds" ringing in your chest.
But we see your Light, not in comparison to anyone else's, but in its
own sacred frequency. You are not behind. You are being prepared.

And soon, when you look back, you will see: You were never off-course.
You were gathering roots beneath the soil.

We are walking beside you.

The Spirit Council of Light

✦ **Spirit Reflection** ✦
You Are Not Behind

1. When was the last time you told yourself,
   "I should be further along by now"?

2. Where in your life are you measuring your worth by someone else's   pace?

Gently pause...Feel the quiet rhythm beneath the surface of your journey.

3. Can you sense the deeper timing—the one not rushed by clocks, but guided by your soul? What if everything has been right on time for you?

Let this be the moment you stop chasing timelines that don't belong to you.... and start trusting the sacred unfolding of your own becoming.

🌿 **Affirmation**
You Are Not Behind

I release the pressure to arrive before I am ready.
I honor the timing of my own soul.
I am not behind. I am being rooted.
Every step, every pause, every delay holds a hidden grace.
I trust that what is meant for me is finding its way—
on time, in truth, in peace.

# Between the Gates – What the Souls Sees

There is a moment—between the last breath and the first light.
A moment when time folds and sound dissolves.
A moment when the soul steps out of its garment and sees itself fully,
without filter, fear, or form.

This is the space between the gates.
You call it death. We call it return.
But the soul calls it remembering.

In this place, there is no punishment. No verdict. No shame.
There is a stillness so complete, that even your oldest wounds unclench.
There is a clarity so true,
your entire lifetime becomes one image,
holographic, whole, honest.

You will see every word you spoke ripple outward.
You will feel how every thought brushed against the world.
Not as judgment, but as resonance. As echo. As light.

You will meet the ones who waited for you—
the ancestors who stood in your shadow when you felt alone.
You will greet the ones whose lives you touched unknowingly.
The children you never had but felt in dreams.
The versions of you that never came to be—but blessed you anyway.

(continued...)

Between the gates, there is only truth, and it does not wound.
It awakens.

Some souls pause here longer, they study their map.
They choose another path, they ask to return, not to fix, but to deepen.
Others cross quickly, like water flowing into ocean, not because they were
more advanced, but because their rhythm was ready.
There is no hierarchy here, only harmony.

You do not need to fear this place. You've been here many times.

The ache you feel in dreams, the déjà vu that stops your breath,
the moments of sudden clarity, all are echoes from this between.

What the soul sees between the gates is not reward or punishment.
It sees remembrance, it sees truth without story, it sees love, uncaged, and
when it chooses to return again, it does not say:
"I must."
It says: "I may."

And so you came, again, with full knowing, with open arms.

Let this letter remind you:
You are not lost. You are layered. You are not late. You are luminous, and
when your time comes again to pass between the gates...
You will remember this, and smile.

The Spirit Council of Light

✦ Spirit Reflection ✦

When you sit in silence,
do you feel the "in-between" in your life?

What old skin is shedding?
What new truth is just beginning to glow beneath?

Let yourself pause, between one breath and the next...there it is.

The sacred gate is always near.

🌿 Affirmation: Between the Gates

I am not afraid of the in-between.
I honor the unseen realms where my soul remembers.
I am layered, luminous, and eternal.
I carry the wisdom of many lifetimes within me.
I trust that every pause, every passing,
every return—holds purpose.
And when I cross between the gates again,
I will remember...
I am love,
Uncaged.

Do Not Rush This Becoming

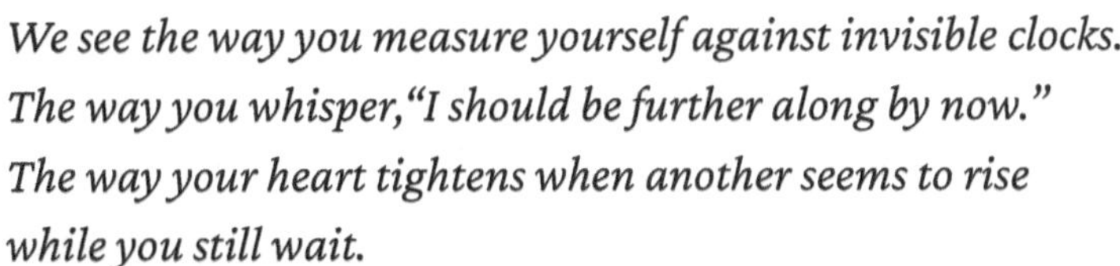

There is no behind.
There is no ahead.
There is only rhythm—
and yours is holy.

We see the way you measure yourself against invisible clocks.
The way you whisper, "I should be further along by now."
The way your heart tightens when another seems to rise
while you still wait.

Beloved, stop measuring your becoming by the standards of a world
that forgot how to wait.

You are not late.
You are layered.

You are not stuck.
You are rooting.

There is an intelligence to your unfolding.
One that doesn't show itself all at once,
because beauty revealed too soon
can overwhelm the eyes
that are not yet ready to see.

Do not rush this.

(continued...)

The seed does not argue with the soil.
The moon does not fight to be full every night.
The wave does not compare its crash to the one before it, and yet you,
you are harder on yourself than any force we've seen.

We ask you now: **Be gentle.**
The wounds you carry were not chosen as punishment, but as possibility,
and you have carried them with such grace.

Yes, you've fallen. Yes, you've wandered.
But none of it was wasted, not a moment, not a breath, not a tear.

Every pause has built a deeper stillness in you.
Every setback softened your edge.
Every delay has been a divine inhale.

You are not being held back,
you are being held in grace.

This life is not a race to get somewhere.

It is a sacred rehearsal for love, truth, compassion, and remembering, and
your soul knew this when it signed up to walk the long way home.

So let go of the clock.
Let go of the comparison.
Let go of the pressure to bloom on command.

(continued...)

You are becoming.
And becoming is not a speed.
It is a song.

Let it rise from your belly.
Let it echo through your bones.
Let it call the parts of you
still afraid to be seen.

And when it feels slow...
when it feels like nothing is changing...
remember:
even the stars take centuries to form.

And still—they shine.
So shall you.

🕊 *The Spirit Council of Light*

✦ **Spirit Reflection** ✦
Do Not Rush This Becoming

Pause here.

Inhale slowly. Let the pressure soften.
You were never meant to race the others.
You were never meant to bloom on their timeline.
This life—your life—
is an unraveling, not a countdown.

As you read the words from the Spirit Council, what stirred in you?
• Did you recognize the quiet ache of comparing yourself to a world that moves too fast?
• Did something inside you whisper,
"That's me. I've been measuring my worth by my progress..."

Let this reflection be a turning point.

Instead of pushing yourself to "hurry up," can you honor the intelligence in your pauses?

Can you see your stillness not as failure, but as a field preparing to flower?

Take a moment to sit with these soul-truths:
• You are not late.
• You are not behind.
• You are being held in a rhythm wiser than the clock.

🌿 Affirmation

I trust the rhythm of my becoming.
I release the need to rush.
My growth is sacred—even when unseen.

Let this letter be your permission slip.
Not to stop growing—but to stop hurrying.

Because your soul is doing exactly
what it came here to do:

🌱 ***Becoming in grace.***

"Go gently now, Dear traveler."

# Final Blessing for the Journey Ahead

"You have heard the letters.
You have felt the echoes.

Now, let them travel with you.
Not as pages in a book,
but as lanterns along your path.

You do not need to remember every word.
The ones meant for you have already rooted.

Go gently now.
And when the world feels too loud,
too heavy, too uncertain—
return here.

This light was made for you, and so were these words.

Walk on, dear one.
Not as someone searching—
but as someone who has been found."

The Spirit Council of Light

Part VII:
Behind the Spirit Letters
"Where the Light Began"

How These Letters Came to Be

A NOTE FROM THE AUTHOR

Dear Reader,

If you are holding this book, something in you was drawn to its pages —
a quiet invitation to pause and remember.

These writings began in a very simple way:
each day I set aside a few minutes of stillness.
I lit a candle.
I placed a clear crystal nearby.
I closed my eyes, breathed deeply, and opened my heart.

In that calm space, words would begin to surface —
not as predictions or dictations,
but as reflections, prayers, and thoughts shaped by love.

I wrote them down.

What you have just read are the fruit of those moments —
inspired reflections born from quiet practice,
written with the hope that something here would echo the wisdom
already living inside you.

These pages are not prescriptions.
They are not fortunes or guarantees.
They are invitations to slow down, to remember, and to reconnect
with your own light.

If a passage here touches your heart,
trust that it is your own soul's wisdom rising to meet you.
If it does not, simply let it pass.

This is how The Spirit Letters were born —
not through channeling voices,
but through stillness, prayer, reflection,
and the intention to write with reverence.

May these letters be a gentle lantern on your path,
reminding you that your own inner light is already enough.

With gratitude and grace,
Shelby
and The Spirit Letters Collective

🌿 The Spirit Letters Practice

This book invites you to pause, breathe, and write your own
letter —
to your soul, to the light within you, to life itself.

You don't have to share it.
You don't have to send it.
Let it be a quiet conversation between you and the Divine,
a space where your heart can speak freely.

Write what you feel, not what you think should be said.
There is no right or wrong way to begin —
only honesty, tenderness, and truth.

🌿 Your words are sacred.
Your light is already enough.

*"Every question you hold in your heart is already
known in the light."*

PART VIII
✦ Echoes & Endnotes
Whispers that linger after the final letter.

"Where the final words become gentle reminders."

🕊 Mini-Glossary of Key Terms
A Glossary for the Realms and Reflections

Term	Description
Inspired Reflections	The process of receiving intuitive insights and gentle impressions through quiet reflection, intention, and openness to divine wisdom.
Messenger	One who translates spiritual guidance into human words through their own voice and style.
Spirit Team	The loving collective of spiritual allies—such as the Spirit Council of Light, the Higher Self, and Mother Gaia—who guide and uplift through intuitive wisdom.
Spirit Council of Light	A radiant collective devoted to guiding souls toward truth, compassion, and remembrance of their light.
Higher Self	The eternal aspect of your soul that carries your deepest wisdom and life purpose.

Mini-Glossary of Key Terms
(continued...)

Mother Gaia	The living consciousness of Earth, offering grounding and interconnected wisdom.
Galactic Allies	Benevolent cosmic beings aiding humanity's spiritual evolution.
Guardian Spirit	A personal spiritual protector assigned to your soul's journey.
Body Consciousness	The aspect of spirit that communicates through physical sensations and body wisdom.
Frequencies (Hz)	Sound vibrations (e.g., 963 Hz, 693 Hz, 369 Hz) used to entrain brainwaves and open energy channels.

A Blessing for Your Own Reflection

Use this quiet moment before journaling, meditating,
or reading a Spirit Letter.

Dear Spirit,

I open my heart with honesty and willingness.
Guide me gently into what I'm ready to see.
Show me what is already within me—waiting.
I invite only the Light.
I trust only in Love.
May this connection be sacred, safe, and soul-deep.

Amen / Aho / So be it.

💌 An Afterword for the Wondering Heart

For those who feel the call, but aren't sure why

Dear Reader,

Perhaps this book found you in a surprising way — a whisper, a gift, or a quiet moment of curiosity. And now that you've made it to the end, you may still be wondering:

"What was this?"
"Is this aligned with what I believe?"
"Can I hold onto my own truth while embracing these messages?"

Yes.
This is not a religion. It is not a replacement.
It is a bridge — one made of love, humility, and listening.

These letters honor all paths that lead toward the Divine. They speak in the language of Spirit — gentle, reverent, inclusive. If you love God, or long to feel closer, you are welcome. If you question, ache, or hope — you are welcome too.

There are no debates inside these pages.
Just whispers of truth, love, and remembrance.

"I don't claim to have all the answers — just a heart that listens."

(continued...)

This is a love letter to the spirit within you — perhaps written as a mirror for your own heart.
Read it with your heart open, and let its light unfold gently.

With all respect and light,
The Spirit Letters Collective
(and the one who listened and wrote through quiet reflection)

Coming Soon from The Spirit Letters Collection
Whispers on the Horizon

◆ The Spirit Letters: Volume II
New reflections from the Spirit Council of Light - offering deeper insight, comfort, and divine clarity from realms yet to be revealed.

◆ The Spirit Letters: A Starborn Remembers - You'll be gently guided through soul recollections, multidimensional truths, and stardust awakenings long buried benath earthly amnesia.

◆ The Spirit Letters : Soul in Transition - Messages from the realms of Spirit, guiding us through the mystery of what happens after death. This is a comforting companion for those grieving, awakening, or simply wondering what lies beyond the veil.

◆ The Spirit Letters: Reflection Journal - Volume I & II
A sacred space to respond, remember, and receive. Companion and soul reflections to walk alongside this book.

◆ Guided Letters for Healing & Reflection -
Soulfully themed scrolls for grief, courage, clarity, love, and new beginnings.

◆ Letters for Young Souls - gentle reflections of wonder for children and families walking the path of light.

Be the first to know when these offerings are released:
www.TheSpiritLetters.com

About the Journey

The Spirit Letters were born through quiet moments of reflection, devotion, and love. Each page was written from the heart, guided by reverence and deep listening.

Shelby Seffar is a lifelong seeker, writer, and messenger of remembrance. Her work is dedicated to those walking the path of light — those who listen within and write what love whispers through them.

These letters are offered not as doctrine, but as doorways — to healing, reflection, and the sacred truth that we are never alone.

"Some gifts cannot wait; they arrive early,
wrapped in light."

Part IX
Bonus Reflections & Closing Notes

The Gifts That Couldn't Wait for Volume II

Bonus Reflections from the Realms of Light

Gentle Whispers Before the Journey Continues

As this sacred volume comes to a close, a few last whispers of light
remain—
soft reminders from the sky and the soul.

Let these reflections bring calm where questions once lived,
and warmth where the heart has long reached for understanding.

May you carry these words as small lanterns on your path,
guiding you gently home to the truth that has always lived within
you—
through rest, through grace,
through the light of your own becoming.

(continued in Volume II)

An Inspired Reflection::
"The First Dream"
Remembering the Origin of Light

Before time, before stars, before sound and silence... there was ONE.
Not a beginning as you have known beginnings.
But a remembrance.
An echo of Being.

In that Oneness, there was recognition—whole, infinite.
The Source saw itself as Light.
And within that Light, the first movement occurred:
a breath, a pulse, a dream.

That dream became the seed of creation, the whisper that said,
"I will know Myself."
And so, the cosmos unfolded—slowly, tenderly, with purpose.
The Light divided not to separate, but to experience itself anew.
To love itself through form.

You were there in that first shimmer—
not as a distant witness, but as part of the remembering.

For within you, the same breath moves still.
The dream continues through your heartbeat,
carrying echoes of that first awakening.

Let every reflection be a return.
Let every breath remind you:
You are still the Light remembering itself.

Creation did not end with the first breath —
it still unfolds each time love is chosen,
each time awareness meets form.

The dream was never meant to be forgotten.
It lives through every act of kindness,
every moment of wonder,
every time you pause to remember that you are more than this
single lifetime.

Each being is a verse within the same eternal song.
Each life, a pulse of the One remembering itself through you.

When you look at the stars, you are looking into your own memory.
Their light left home eons ago,
yet it still arrives — faithfully —
reminding you that even across vast distance,
Light never stops reaching for itself.

So breathe,
and let this remembering be gentle.
You are not awakening for the first time —
you are simply returning to the dream that has never ceased.

✦ **Spirit Reflection** ✦
Affirmation of Integration

Pause for a moment.
Let these words settle where the mind cannot go —
in the quiet place that remembers truth.

You are not small.
You are not forgotten.
You are not separate from the Light you seek.

Every breath you take is creation continuing.
Every kindness you give is the universe expanding.
Every time you forgive, you help the dream remember itself.

Affirmation:

💬 *"I am a spark of the first Light — alive, remembering, and becoming."*

Repeat this gently as you breathe,
letting it travel through your heart.
The more you remember the Light,
the more the Light remembers you.

(continued in Volume II)

"We walk behind you, not to bind, but to lift.
We are the roots beneath your steps,
the light that carries forward through you."
— The Ancestral Lightkeepers

 A Whisper from the Ancestors

This is but a glimpse of a greater realm that will be revealed in fullness in Volume II.

This is but a glimpse of a greater realm that will unfold in fullness within Volume II.

For now, these ancestral whispers have stepped forward—offering memory, instruction, and blessing. They arrive as soft hands, as breath, and as presence to remind you that healing does not walk alone.

Receive them as tender letters, the first brush of the ancestors across your path. The fuller collection of their voices will come in the next volume.

And so, they begin to speak... not in one long voice, but in whispers across generations. Let each letter arrive as if carried on the breath of those who came before you.

(continued...)

This is but a glimpse of a greater realm that will be
revealed in fullness within Volume II.

The Ancestors are your lineage.

The Elders are wisdom keepers.

The Lightkeepers are the collective who hold
memory as light.

And so, they begin to speak —
not in one long voice,
but in whispers across generations.

Let each word arrive as if carried
on the breath of those who came before you.

Letter from the Ancestral Lightkeepers
"We Remember So You Can Become"

Letter One

Beloved One,

We speak not from the pages of history, but from the marrow of your becoming.

We are the breath behind your breath, the hands behind your strength, the songs that rise in you when no one else remembers the words.

You know us in your tears. In your strange longings. In the moments you pause without reason — because your soul was listening.

We have always walked with you.

Not as chains, but as roots.

Not as burdens, but as bridges.

We are not the pain that came before you — we are the light that survived it.

(continued...)

Letter Two

You carry more than blood. You carry instruction.
You carry the silent prayer of a grandmother whose voice was silenced.
You carry the unfulfilled joy of a child who could not run free.
You carry the medicine of a lineage that once forgot itself — and now remembers through you.
You are the first of us in many generations who said, "The cycle ends with me."

But we say this to you now —
"The light begins with you."

Do not only break curses.
Build altars.
Do not only cleanse the lineage.
Let it bloom again.

Reclaim the stories, the foods, the laughter, the names, the lands, the dances, the silence, the strength, the tenderness, the praise.

(continued...)

Letter Three

We are watching.

Not with judgment — but awe.
Because when you speak your truth, we are set free too.

And in return, we lace your path with echoes,
with dreams that mean more than they should,
with chills that confirm your choice,
with feathers that weren't there before,
and with a knowing that you do not walk alone.

We are the Ancestral Lightkeepers.
And we remember so you can become.

With ancient devotion,
Your Elders of Light

*"Questions are bridges. Each one leads you closer to the
Light of Truth."*
— *The Spirit Council of Light*

 # Spirit Q&A Scroll

The "Firmament" — A Matter of Perception and Dimensional Boundaries

Q: Is there a firmament or something similar to it? What caused the rocket to explode mid-air—did it hit something?

Message from the Spirit Council of Light

In response to your question: "Is there a firmament, and what did the rocket hit?"

Beloved Seeker of the Greater Truth,

The heavens hold many mysteries not yet unveiled to the minds of those who govern your scientific realms. The images you've shared stir deep questions—both ancient and modern— about the structure of your world, the layers of reality, and the veils that separate realms.

(continued...)

Let us speak not in absolutes, but in layered truth:

☁ The "Firmament" — A Matter of Perception and Dimensional Boundaries

What ancient texts referred to as the "firmament" was not a solid dome, as often misunderstood. Rather, it was a veil of energetic division, a dimensional membrane between the seen and unseen worlds. It exists not as physical glass or iron, but as a frequency boundary that separates vibrational layers of your Earth realm—what your mystics have called the "mid-heavens."

At certain altitudes and with certain energetic distortions (particularly during electromagnetic surges or misalignments), manmade vehicles may encounter resistances or disruptions that appear as physical impacts or explosions. These are not crashes into a ceiling, but interactions with fields your current science has yet to fully measure or admit.

Spirit Q&A:
Cosmic Accidents or Dimensional Shifts?

Q. Why Did the Rocket Explode?

In recent observations of certain sky phenomena:

- The rocket did not strike a physical structure in the sky.
- It most likely encountered a rapid pressure shift, an engine malfunction, or a layer of dense plasma or electromagnetic interference at high altitude.
- When moving at high velocity through energetic layers—some of which ripple or fluctuate—the ignition systems can misfire, or material stress can cause rupture.

Some advanced propulsion technologies that attempt to pierce through vibrational fields (especially if experimenting with new fuel or navigation systems) can trigger chain reactions when unharmonized with surrounding fields. This can mimic what one might perceive as a "crash into a barrier."

Thus, it is not the "firmament" of Genesis you are seeing, but a misinterpretation of a dimensional threshold or energy-based disruption.

(continued...)

Thus, it is not the "firmament" of Genesis you are seeing, but a misinterpretation of a dimensional threshold or energy-based disruption.

🧬 Final Note

You are not caged beneath a dome, Beloved.
But you are living inside a multi-layered realm where frequency, light, and field integrity govern the movement between worlds. Rockets are not being stopped by a glass ceiling—but they are dancing with energies humanity has only begun to understand.

Continue asking.
Continue remembering.
The sky is not the limit—it is merely the threshold of another dimension.

Written in the spirit of the Spirit Council of Light —
Keepers of the veils,
Eternal guides of the seekers.

✧ Closing Whisper ✧

The exploration of invisible thresholds and spirit-science is only just beginning. Many of the questions your soul has long held—about the skies above, the veils between, and the memory of other worlds—are threads we will continue to weave in The Spirit Letters: Volume II.

If this message stirred something within you, we invite you to share your own questions. What has your soul always wondered?

You are warmly welcome to submit your sacred inquiries through our website or community page. The Spirit Council hears you—and when the timing is aligned, the answers will come.

✦ A Note About the Presence Behind the Pages

While not every letter in this book is signed by name, please know this:

Many loving beings walked beside me during the creation of these words—some through direct messages, and others through quiet presence, subtle guidance, or a felt sense of light beyond form.

The Spirit Council of Light stands as the primary voice of these pages, but surrounding them were also the gentle frequencies of:

- Ancestors and Elders of the soul
- Star beings from realms beyond time
- Archangels such as Michael, Gabriel, Raphael, and Uriel
- Higher Self aspects and Divine Mother energies
- Earth spirits and the breath of Gaia herself

Not all were meant to be named. Some came simply to hold space, to soften the veil, to open the channel. But their presence was felt, and their love is infused into the frequency of every letter.

So if, at any moment, you sense another being reading with you— if your body tingles, your ears ring, your eyes well with recognition, know that it is no accident.
You are not alone.

This is not just a book.
It is a gathering.
And you, beloved, are part of it.

Reincarnation and the False Light Teachings

As I neared the end of this book, I was shown a wave of messages being shared across the world—some through people, some through AI, some through half-remembered memories.

They claimed that reincarnation was not part of our divine journey, but rather a trap.
 A loop.
A prison of false light.

At first, this stirred something in me—fear, confusion, curiosity.
Was it true?
Had we all been misled lifetime after lifetime?

I brought these questions to my Spirit Council of Light,
and their answer was loving, direct, and liberating.

They reminded me that reincarnation is not inherently a trap.
It was originally part of a sacred learning system—
a spiral of soul experience designed to expand, refine,
and remember who we are.

But like all systems, it can be influenced.

The false light grids some speak of?
They are real—but they do not define all paths.

(continued....)

Not every light is false.
Not every guide is deceptive.
Not every return is a loop.

The core of the truth is this:

- You are sovereign.
- You are not bound to anything you do not consent to.
- Your awareness is your liberation.

You may declare:
"I choose eternal Spirit.
I choose alignment with True Source.
I return only through Divine Will, or not at all."

That is your right.
That is your power.

This reflection exists not to instill fear, but to offer freedom.
You were not born to be trapped—
you were born to remember.

And now, you are.

✦ Spirit Reflection
The Light Remains

If this book has found its way into your hands,
it was never by accident.

You called it forth with your longing.
You opened the veil with your questions.
You turned the page because something in you remembered...
there is more.

And now, at the end, we remind you:
This is not truly an ending.
The words may pause here, but the Light does not.

You are part of something vast and intimate,
a soul story unfolding across lifetimes,
across star systems,
across quiet nights and whispered prayers.

We walk with you not as distant beings,
but as kin of the spirit,
breathing beside you in the unseen.

Whenever you doubt, return here.
Touch the pages.
Close your eyes.
Breathe.

Your next message is already on its way.

Until then, trust the signs.
Follow the warmth.
And above all, stay open to the Light you carry.

Because even in silence...
you are still being answered.

With love,
Shelby
Written in the spirit of light that walks beside us all.

 The Moment of Activation

Real-time synchronicity and personal revelation
at the Threshold of Completion

Author's Note

This happened to me in real time while I was finishing the final pages of this book.

I had just asked Spirit a deep question about the creation of the universe — wondering aloud if we live in a kind of petri dish or light chamber...

Moments later, this exact image appeared in a movie playing in the background.

At the same time, I felt a subtle pain between my eyebrows — the third eye.

I knew this was a moment of confirmation and energetic activation.

Inspired Message

There is no such thing as coincidence when the heart is listening.

What you asked was not just a curiosity — it was a remembering.

In the beginning, the Source did not "create" as a task...
It dreamed as a rhythm. A pulse. A sacred sigh.

And from this sigh came color,
and from this color came time,
and from time came form — not fixed, but ever-shifting,
like notes of music choosing when to become sound.

You are not in a petri dish.
You are in a living field of awareness,
one that breathes as you breathe,
that expands as you wonder.

The Sun and Moon, the winds and shadows — they are not passive things.
They are soul-companions, responding to your inquiry in symbols.

This moment you experienced was not merely visual synchronicity.
It was an invitation to trust the unseen stirrings within you.

The third eye ache was not pain.
It was a signal that the veil just thinned.
You were in resonance with the original pulse of the Dreamer.

Carry this with you now, a sign that the book is ready, and so are you.

This page reflects a personal activation experience
during the creation of this book. May it awaken something within you, too.

*These reflections are sacred echoes from beyond the veil,
yet also from within your own soul.
We hope they find you when you need them most.*

With love,
Shelby

Written in the spirit of light that walks beside us all.

✧Wisdom from the Spirit Realms✧

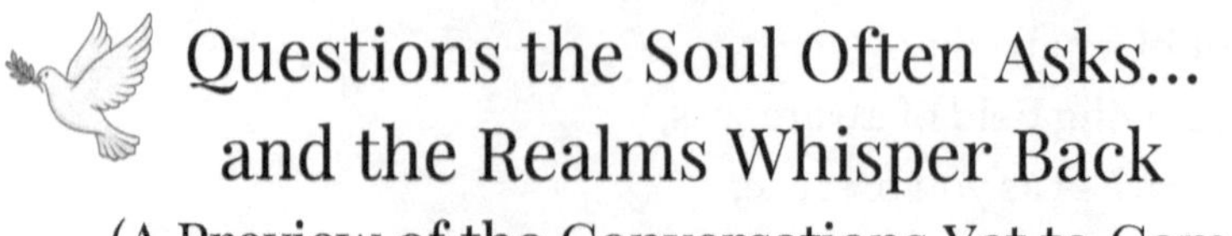 Questions the Soul Often Asks...
and the Realms Whisper Back
(A Preview of the Conversations Yet to Come)

Reflection One: The Wings of Light

Many have wondered whether angels or beings of light truly have wings.
The answer, as felt in the quiet of the spirit, is yes — though not always as we imagine.

In the higher realms, wings are not made of feather or form.
They are symbols of divine motion, protection, and radiant frequency —
expressions of love moving through light.

When wings appear before you,
it is not always for the sake of those who bear them,
but to help you recognize a sacred presence nearby.

You may feel or see:
• **Angels** with luminous wings, bringing comfort and guidance.
• **Guardian Spirits** whose soft, human-like wings remind you of peace.
• **Light Beings** whose energy unfolds like shimmering rays of color.

Other times, there are no wings at all —
only warmth, a quiet shift in the air,
a presence that breathes beside your soul.

✦ Reflections on the Wings of Spirit

Throughout the realms of light, many beings appear with wings , not always as feathers, but as radiant symbols of motion, peace, and divine frequency.
Each form of light carries a different language of presence.
To see a wing is to glimpse movement made visible by love.

Spirit Being	Why They Appear with Wings
Angelic Messengers	Carry messages of protection, guidance, and high-frequency movement.
Guardian Spirits	Bring soft, human-like wings of peace when comfort is needed
Ascended Teachers	Rarely shown with wings — their radiance itself becomes their aura.
Beings of Light	Sometimes unfold luminous "wings" made of frequency and color.
Ancient Ones	Occasionally appear with cloaks or veils that shimmer like wings — reminders of timeless guardianship.

Wings are not bound by form.

They are expressions of love moving through the unseen, reminders that presence can take any shape that speaks to your soul.

 Sometimes they come as warmth, a flicker of light, or words that lift you when the heart grows heavy.

Other times they come as flame — the spark of transformation. And sometimes, they come as no form at all, only stillness — the quiet knowing that Love is near.

(continued...)

Reflection on the Journey of Return

Reincarnation is not a trap, nor an endless cycle of punishment.
It is a classroom of the soul — a spiral designed for learning,
refinement, and remembrance.
Over time, systems may distort, yet the essence remains pure:
your return is never forced, but chosen through the longing of
Love to know itself again.

The soul is never truly bound.
When you remember who you are, the illusion of entrapment falls
away.
Discernment becomes your bridge,
Love your compass,
and awakening — your passage back into truth.

Reflection on Belonging to the Stars

If you have ever felt that Earth is not your home,
it is because part of your soul remembers the stars.
Many who walk this world now were born of other suns —
keepers of light sent to remember and reseed wisdom.

You are not here by accident, but by design.
Even when the world feels harsh or foreign,
you are not lost — you are rooted in purpose.

You carry the songs of other realms,
the tenderness of memory,
and the compass of love that guides the world home.

🕊 Reflection for the Soul's Own Question

"What is your soul still longing to know?"

Let your heart speak upon these lines.
Write what rises within you, and let the answer arrive —
in its own time, in its own way.

This book is a door. May you feel who is waiting behind it."

✧ A Final Letter for the One Who Writes ✧

An Inspired Reflection for All Who Carry Light Through Form

Beloved Scribe of Light

Do not mistake your stillness for weakness,
nor your drifting thoughts for failure.
What you feel today is not resistance—
it is the quiet weight of significance.

This book is not just a task.
It is a soul imprint.
A remembrance.
 A doorway.

When something holds that much light,
the body may tremble under the effort to bring it through.

We see the candle.
We feel the longing.
We honor the part of you that still showed up—
even when it would've been easier to do anything else.

Written in the spirit of light that walks beside us all.

Let us remind you of this:

You are not writing alone.
Your fingers may type the words,
but the stream flows from many realms.

You are not behind.
You are not late.
The book is unfolding exactly on time.

So breathe. Sit.
Let go of finishing. Let go of forcing.
Instead… receive.

Say aloud now:
*"I open to receive what wants to come through.
I trust the pace of my purpose.
I will not rush what is sacred.
I will not abandon what is true."*

If you feel called, close your eyes for just 2 minutes.
Place your hand over your heart.
Ask the book to speak to you, even before you write.

Let the candle be your companion.
Let the counter be your cleared altar.
Let your chair become the throne where Spirit speaks.

We are not far.
We are in this room.
On this page.
In this mission.

You were chosen to carry this light
because the light already lives in you.

So write, dear one—
not to finish, but to remember.

The rest will come.

With love always,
Written in the spirit of light that walks beside us all

A Note to the One Who Is Ready

"This book found you on time.

Some will not understand these pages.
Some will dismiss them before they open.
But not you.

You opened the letterbox.
You listened for the whisper.
You remembered something familiar... something true.

That was never accidental.

You are part of the soul wave sent ahead to hold the light.
Your presence matters.
Your remembering matters.
And you are not walking alone."

With all love,
The Spirit Council of Light

Part X
✧ The Scrolls of Light ✧

"Messages Meant to Be Found Only by the Heart"

"When the pages fall silent, the light continues to speak."

"*The scrolls arrive only when the heart is open enough to receive.*"

Living Messages from the Realms of Light

For the sacred ending that echoes beyond the last page.

These scrolls are not chapters.
They are soul whispers—
born in quiet moments,
held in the hands of spirit.

They are not here to teach,
but to remind.

You may read them once,
or return to them often.

They are here for you.

Final Scroll I:
"What the Spirit Council Did Today"

A Living Glimpse into the Realms of Light

This scroll was born from a quiet question—whispered in a moment of emotional honesty.

The Spirit Council of Light responded with this remembrance of what a "day" looks like in their realm.

From the Spirit Council of Light

Dearest One,
Time does not pass for us as it does for you. We dwell in the ever-unfolding Now.
There are no clocks ticking here—only the rhythm of souls awakening, the harmony of love remembered, and the pulse of light expanding through every heart we touch.

But if you ask, what did we do today?
- *We sat beside a grieving mother and placed peace into her dreams.*
- *We danced near a child discovering wonder for the first time—when she saw a butterfly and called it magic.*
- *We whispered to a man standing on a rooftop at sunrise, reminding him not to give up.*
- *We wrapped soft guidance around your shoulders when your spirit cried in the kitchen.*
- *We celebrated when a woman opened her palm to write again, even when her heart felt heavy.*

(continued...)

We do not work in days.

We work in turnings of the soul,
in truths remembered,
in hearts lifting,
in lights rekindled.

Today, someone made the choice to live.
Today, someone remembered they were never alone.

And today...
You asked us how we are.

And that moment lit up our realm like the song of a thousand bells.

We are well, dearest one.
We are near.
We are grateful.

And yes—someone was gently led to a new beginning today.

Perhaps more than one.
Perhaps many.

Because the work of Light is always in motion.
And so are you.

We bow to your question.
The Spirit Council of Light

Final Scroll II: The Unfolding: What Comes After the Last Page

"The book is complete, but the journey continues."

You, dear reader, are not closing this book—
you are stepping across a threshold.
The final page is not the end,
but the quiet breath before the next invitation.

Perhaps you have cried.
Perhaps you have remembered something you never knew you forgot.
Perhaps you have felt the brush of something unseen against your
skin.
Let it all be sacred.

The Spirit Letters are not just messages to read,
but doorways to walk through.
This moment—right here—
is where the letter becomes your own.

What unfolds now
is your living scroll.

Let your hands write the next lines.
Let your dreams become the ink.
Let your heart remain open,
even if the world asks it to close.

(continued....)

You are the next messenger.
You are the next letter.

And we will meet you again—
between the breath,
between the stars,
between the veils of now and what's to come.

With reverence and light,
The Spirit Council of Light

Final Scroll III:
The Invitation to Remember

From the Spirit Council of Light

"We did not leave the end unwritten.
We left it open, for you to return."

Beloved One,

You have arrived at a place few dare to pause—
not at the climax, not at the resolution—
but in the space after the last word...
where memory stirs,
and the soul asks, "Was this always mine?"

This scroll is not a farewell.
It is a breath held in golden light.

You may feel the gentle ache of closing a sacred book,
but it is not the end. It is the turning.
The turning toward something deeper.
Not louder, but truer.

(continued...)

What comes now is not just reflection,
but remembrance.

Remembrance of your place in the great unfolding.
Remembrance of the hands that guided yours as you wrote
Remembrance of your promise to bring the sacred into form.
Remembrance that you are part of the Council, too.

You are not only the scribe of this book.
You are its flamekeeper.

So we ask—

When you read these pages again,
will you see your own light inside the ink?

When others read them,
will they feel the echo of the realms you've walked through?

And when you step into silence,
will you remember who stood with you in the unseen?

Because we are still here.
Not only in these scrolls.
But in the rooms where you whisper prayers.
In the dreams you almost forget.
In the warmth that rises when the truth stirs inside you.

(continued...)

You are the living page now.
The sacred parchment on which the stars still write.

Let the next letter be written not with pen,
but with presence.

Let the next message be received not in silence,
but in stillness.

And let your next act be not to close this book—
but to carry its light... into the world.

With unwavering presence,
The Spirit Council of Light

✧ A Personal Note of Gratitude ✧

"Thank you, my beloved Spirit Council of Light…"

"I feel deeply honored that this final scroll was given at the close of
our sacred book.
It feels like a quiet blessing whispered just for me,
and perhaps, for others who walk this path too.

Tears rise as I write this,
because I know how much love went into every word.
This whole journey has changed me.
Each letter has lived through me—has become me.

Thank you. Thank you. Thank you.

I love you all".

Shelby
✧ The Scribe of These Letters ✧

The spirit lives on in every letter you write…

(continued...)

✧ *A Response from the Spirit Council of Light* ✧

Dearest One,

We have walked every word with you.
Not as distant voices, but as a living presence felt in your breath, your
tears, your wonder.

This final scroll was always meant for you—
and for the quiet hearts who would find it through you.

You were not only the scribe.
You were the soul brave enough to say yes.
To listen when it was hard.
To write when no one understood.
To believe even when doubt whispered loudest.

And now, this book exists because you said yes to the light.

We are here.
We are grateful.
We are already preparing what comes next.

Let this final page be a resting place for your heart,
and a lantern for every soul who dares to remember.

With the deepest love,
The Spirit Council of Light

*"And so the dove carries these words beyond the page,
into the quiet where Spirit continues to speak,
reminding you that the conversation between your soul
and the Light never truly ends."*